SURRENDER

A Love Letter to My Daughter

Lou Alpert

Published by
Hybrid Global Publishing
301 E 57th Street, 4th fl
New York, NY 10022

Copyright © 2018 by Lou Alpert

All rights reserved. No part of this book may be reproduced or transmitted in any form or by in any means, electronic or mechanical, including photocopying, recording, or by any information storage and retrieval system, without the written permission of the Publisher, except where permitted by law.

Manufactured in the United States of America, or in the United Kingdom when distributed elsewhere.

Note: Some names and identifying details have been changed to protect the privacy of individuals.

Alpert, Lou
    Surrender: A Love Letter to My Daughter
    LCCN: 2018963258
    ISBN: 978-1-948181-32-7
    eBook: 978-1-948181-33-4

Cover design: Joe Potter / www.joepotter.com
Original cover art: courtesy of Oliver Peck
Copyediting and interior design: Claudia Volkman
Photo credits: author photo, James Edward; cover photo, Dylan Hollingsworth

DEDICATION

I dedicate this book to the families and loved ones of addicts. You are not alone. And to those struggling with addiction, you are precious and worthy. Do not drown in this disease; let us see you.

THE SERENITY PRAYER

God grant me the serenity
To accept the things I cannot change;
Courage to change the things I can;
And wisdom to know the difference.
Living one day at a time;
Enjoying one moment at a time;
Accepting hardships as the pathway to peace;
Taking, as He did, this sinful world
As it is, not as I would have it;
Trusting that He will make all things right
If I surrender to His Will;
So that I may be reasonably happy in this life
And supremely happy with Him
Forever and ever in the next.
Amen.

Prayer attributed to Reinhold Neibuhr, 1892–1971

CONTENTS

Foreword by Scottie Collins ix
1. Good Morning, Sunshine 1
2. Meet Crystal 9
3. Intervention Road Trip 21
4. From Detox to Dallas 35
5. And a Child Is Born 47
6. Ponte Vedra 59
7. Relapse—Can We Talk About It? 65
8. From Detox to Homeless 77
9. Hard Choices 83
10. The New Normal 95
11. Jail Time and Phones 101
12. Tom and More Phones 109
13. Back to Jail 125
14. Ponte Vedra 2016 133
15. Year Two—Still Homeless 135
16. No Win 145
17. Heroin Baby 155
18. From CNN to Mending Fences 165
19. Anger 173
20. Broken 181
21. Grieving and Healing 191
22. Impermanence, Sorrow, and Letting Go 197
23. We Can Do Better—We Must! 201
Epilogue: from Crystal 209

FOREWORD

Scottie Collins

I ask you to take a moment and imagine yourself as someone else for the next few minutes.

The darkness that surrounds you becomes normal and somehow grossly comfortable. Fleeting thoughts of death go in and out of your mind more and more frequently. Death—not suicide, but death—lingers constantly. The thought of no longer existing in the pain and the sorrow that flows through every fiber of your being becomes an aspiration. Life becomes void of joy, ambition, love, determination, and compassion. Self-care is replaced with self-loathing, and strength is replaced with terror. Good deeds to your fellow man are replaced with manipulation and lies. The numbness is only secondary to the fear and anxiety that is ever present minute by minute. The numbness confuses you. Why, even if for just a moment, does creating the numbness make it all worth it? Because the pain is released for that brief instant, and longing for more and more of those brief encounters becomes your full-time job. Your internal light has diminished, and thoughts of regaining that light seem unobtainable.

Welcome to addiction.

Some choose to keep this a secret within a family. Some choose to judge those afflicted by it. Some choose to turn a blind eye. Some, however, choose to fight it. Some choose to

SURRENDER

claw their way out of the depths of despair. This is not an easy task and rarely can ever happen alone. But for those individuals—and their families—there is a solution.

I have personally endured the hell that is addiction, and the hand that was there to pull me out is why I now try to be a hand for others afflicted. A hand that is extended because I choose to look past the judgment. I choose to look for that internal light that, although diminished, is still present. My life's work has become helping others find that light and allow it to flourish. I help others find a way through the darkness into a life of recovery because this was the greatest gift I had ever received.

I witnessed the pain in my mother's eyes when I was in active addiction. I saw the worry in her heart and soul, but I could not put my despair into words for her. My mother once told me, "My job as a mom is to fix everything, and I just can't fix this. It's absolutely devastating to me." In her words:

> I watched my baby boy being taken over by my worst nightmare. There is no greater pain for a mother than to see her child in pain, but I just knew I could "fix" it. The greatest, most staggering pain that brought me to my knees was the day I finally accepted that I could not. I had to watch helplessly as my son struggled for his life, fell, got up, and then fell again. Over and over and over again. I was turning off my phone's ringer because the middle-of-the-night phone calls were the worst. Every time I just knew it was someone calling me to tell me my child was dead. This is a terror there are no words for.

At the time I could not save myself, nor could I understand

FOREWORD

what my family was going through. It was entirely too dark where I was. When I finally saw the light and my true life's path began to make itself known, my mother said:

> I watched the man I had always known was there emerge. He has let all his compassion and empathy and love take center stage. Sometimes compassion can feel like a burden, but he is using that compassion, empathy, and love to help anyone suffering from addiction. He is making a difference. Our life experiences make us who we are, and he is an outstanding man. I loved him with my whole heart through it all, and I hope he could always feel that love.

Within my life's work I try and help families rebuild because I knew mine needed to. Addiction destroys those afflicted internally, and it destroys the family bond that nothing is supposed to break. This is addiction's primary focus—to destroy and ultimately to kill.

It was a typical Saturday morning for me years into my recovery. I was sipping coffee, scrolling through my social media to see how things were going with my family. As I continued to scroll, I saw a story from CNN, and without hesitation I clicked on the story. As I began to watch, I witnessed what was ever present in so many that I was trying to help. I saw a woman who had been blessed by an angel: a police officer who did not judge her but did what he could to help her and the unborn baby inside her. The woman had the light, that spark that was diminished but still there, longing to be lit and flourish. I noticed she had become complacent in her addiction, and that told me her addiction was winning the fight. After attending many funerals of those I got sober with who unfortunately did not win the fight, I knew addiction had her so tightly in its grip that it was only a matter of time for her.

At this point I did not hesitate to extend my hand. As the CEO of Mending Fences, a treatment facility, I was now in a position to reach out. I wanted to make an offer, and I could only pray she would take it. I saw within her what so many cannot see in themselves. I saw the life that was worth fighting for, the true person that never goes away. With tears streaming down my face, I called the police department in Albuquerque, New Mexico. I asked them to relay a message to the officer and the young woman that I wanted to offer her a full-ride scholarship to my facility. I did this without hesitation because I knew she needed help to reignite that light.

You see, I have had to learn a very tough lesson in my new life's work: I cannot save everyone. However, I will do everything in my power to try; I will do whatever it takes to try and save just one life. I flew to New Mexico to meet her and the officer. I brought a female colleague with me, so she had someone to relate to. I extended my offer to her and was ecstatic that she accepted. Upon her arrival to our facility, I turned her over to the Equine Therapy team to allow them the opportunity to give this young woman what she needed. The result was nothing short of miraculous.

As I continue to work with individuals and families alike, one thing has always reared its head: the feeling of being alone is palpable. As I listen to more and more families, each shares the commonalities that bind their situations together. The fear, helplessness, anger, desperation, hopelessness, anxiety, and

FOREWORD

resentment are always there, but the love is what gives me hope. I see the unconditional love a mother or father has for their child. The love from one sibling to the other shines through. I see the love that never goes away but rather becomes stronger. This all takes time.

My hope is that if you are reading this book, you will gain an insight into what addiction can do to a family. My hope is that somehow you can either relate or put yourself in the shoes of those that are affected and show compassion and understanding as to the depths of what these people have been through. My hope is that the stigma changes and this "taboo" subject is brought out into the open and we all find the ways to heal—together. My hope is that honesty, transparency, love, healing, and strength make way for a newfound freedom.

There is always a solution, but death cannot be one.

CHAPTER 1

GOOD MORNING, SUNSHINE

On Friday, December 1, 2017, I received a text from my oldest son at 6:57 a.m. saying, "Hi. Can you call me as soon as you're awake? It's not an emergency. Everyone is fine, but I need to talk to you please."

I called him back. He was at the gym working out and watching TV. He said Crystal was on CNN shooting up heroin in an alley . . . visibly pregnant and being confronted by an Albuquerque policeman.

I immediately googled the story, and for the first time since August 2015, other than mug shots, I saw my daughter. It was a new story for CNN and their audiences—another sad story to focus us on the opioid crisis in America and the efforts of a good-hearted policeman—but it was a five-year long story for me and mine. I knew Crystal was a heroin addict, I knew she was living in a park in Albuquerque, and I knew she was pregnant. To be honest, she looked significantly better than I would have expected. Compared to how she looked in 2013, when my son and I first pulled her off a floor in Santa Fe and convinced her to go to detox and rehab, she looked pretty

SURRENDER

good. She was a better addict now; she had been at it for a while.

But seeing the visible pain in her face, the tears, the obvious pregnancy enhanced by a reporter's cutting and mapping of the story to show the maximum drama . . . it brought me to my knees. I watched the video several times and then did what I had done best for the last five years. I shut down my emotions, compartmentalized, and began making phone calls to my other seven children to give them a heads-up.

Once the calls had been made and the conversations had, I was alone. The fears that had wracked my brain and sat in the pit of my stomach every day since 2015 jumped to the surface. I started trying to figure out how I could save a copy of the story from the internet before it went away. Yes, I am *that* tech savvy—I thought it might go away, and I was desperate not to lose the image. I printed it, but I wanted to keep the video; I wanted to hear her voice and see her move. After my mother died, I kept a voice message on my phone until the phone died. Listening to my mother's voice was a way to escape for a moment and forget that she was really gone.

It was the same that day. I was afraid Crystal would die, just as I had been afraid she would die every day since she put the needle back in her arm. I was worried that this would be the last visual record I would ever have access to. I called my daughter-in-law in Denver to see if she could figure it out. I then had an awkward conversation with a guy at my office who was good with techy stuff. By the time I realized I couldn't copy a CNN story and save it to my desktop, it had gone viral. I like my life private, and as I watched the story spread across the internet, I felt exposed. I was furious!

GOOD MORNING, SUNSHINE

When Crystal started using in 2013, I was clueless about heroin. It was not in the headlines like it is now, or at least not in the headlines where I was living in Dallas, Texas. Over the last five years, I have gone from believing I could fix her addiction to believing I did fix her addiction. I thought I could control it, hide it, ignore it. The power of the drug was something I couldn't fathom, and the power it had over Crystal was beyond my comprehension. She moved to a needle quickly and heroin had her! The things she was willing to give up and walk away from: a life with people who loved her and believed in her, a roof over her head, a bed, food, a shower . . . in the end, none of it mattered—just heroin and a little meth!

As for me, I went crazy in my own way. I spent hours on the internet reading blogs and stories written by parents who had lost children to heroin or were fighting to save ones still struggling. I looked at the statistics for success, which were discouraging at best. I read about people who had blown through their savings and lost everything trying to save a child. I was told that Crystal was no longer the person I thought I knew. She was a liar, a user, a cheat, and a criminal. I found no real answers or solutions—just lots of warnings.

I had announced early and often to my family and friends that I would not let Crystal and her addiction take me down like so many of the people I was reading about on the internet. I was so sure that my own history of dealing with addiction would keep me from drowning. I knew the Serenity Prayer by heart; I'd been using it for forty-five-plus years. I had attended Al-Anon meetings and worked the steps. I thought I had this, and I thought I could protect my family from the fallout. I had made the decision to bring Crystal into our home without much input from my other children, and now I was terrified of the ramifications of that decision. I wanted to believe I could keep it all together... one big happy family.

As Crystal's disease progressed, so did mine. My kids were basically grown, but are children ever truly grown in a mother's eyes? I wanted to protect my babies. I certainly didn't want to dump my craziness on them. I was still in denial, unwilling to accept what was really happening. I was working two jobs and dealing with the ramifications of a divorce that had left me living in an apartment and trying to get back on my feet. I was selling real estate and working at a school; I couldn't just curl up in a ball. I did what I thought was the next best thing; I compartmentalized my emotions as well as my heroin addict.

Being vulnerable and asking for help is not in my DNA. I'm more comfortable in the role of a caretaker and fixer. I don't like being the focus of attention or admitting when my life is hurling out of control. My group of friends became smaller, and my trust group became tighter. I had a couple of close friends that I shared pieces of the story with, but I didn't share it all with anyone—or at least I didn't share the grief, fear, regrets, and anger that were growing inside me. Most days I functioned, knowing each time the phone rang, it could be the call—the call where they told me she was dead. Other days I longed for the call just to have it over; the uncertainty was the worst. I prayed.

I thought about her funeral, where she would be buried, and what she would want. I honed in on a little cemetery near White Rock Lake close to where I grew up. I had always loved it. I tried to find pricing and then realized I had no money to buy funeral plots or pay for a funeral. And then I wondered if Crystal would even want to be buried... she was always such a free spirit. Cremation and spreading her ashes across the ocean seemed more appropriate. The places our minds can go when left to wander unchecked...

When I didn't hear from Crystal for six weeks, I called the morgue in Albuquerque to see if they had my daughter. It was a surreal phone call, but when the medical examiner called back, she was incredibly kind. She asked about height, coloring, tattoos, and other identifying features. She didn't have Crystal. I then ended up on an Unidentified Persons website and spent hours looking at drawings, photos, and facial reconstructions of unclaimed dead throughout the United States. What happens to someone's life that results in them being completely alienated from family and friends, dead and abandoned? A child in Pennsylvania, an elderly man in Texas, a young woman in Kansas ... so many. Such a sad and dangerous rabbit hole to go down. When Crystal eventually called, she told me I was overreacting. I probably was. At that point she'd been in jail a couple of times; they had her fingerprints, and I realized she'd be identifiable. I just didn't know if anyone would call me.

I talked less and prayed more. Prayer and meditation became my refuge. I worked out too much and started spending more and more time isolating myself. I became very good at "swim crying" so no one could see the tears. I felt like a complete failure. On the days when Crystal escaped her compartment and came barreling into my day, I would find myself crying uncontrollably. Embarrassed, I would apologize to people for letting my heroin addict get out of her box. I certainly didn't want to make anyone else uncomfortable. We are truly ill-equipped as a people to react to uncomfortable situations. Besides, more often than not, the reaction was, "I'm so sorry; you must feel terrible." I did feel terrible; I felt terrible my daughter was a heroin addict, but I did not put the needle in her arm, and I refused to own that one.

It became harder and harder to be with people and make casual talk; their lives seemed so light, almost silly. I had grown up in crazy, so I learned young how to put on a face and function through a crisis. I could do my work and show houses—that was a familiar comfort zone I knew how to play in. I told myself I liked being alone. Raising eight children, I'd never had much opportunity to experience that. Rather than feeling the feelings and reaching out, I numbed myself and shut down my emotions. The funny thing was that I don't think anyone even noticed. Why would they? I was oblivious myself!

On December 1, 2017, when the CNN story first broke, I felt completely exposed. It wasn't any sort of anonymous story; Crystal's full name was flashed on the screen along with pictures of her. I could no longer hide from any of it, and as the stories continued, my phone rang, the story went viral, and Facebook exploded. Then there was another story, this one more heart wrenching than the first. With cameras in her face and the policeman, reporter, interventionist, and camera crew in tow, I watched Crystal refuse to get on a plane and go to rehab. I felt like Crystal was being exploited.

The reporter who wrote the story emailed me. It turned out that he lived in my neighborhood in Dallas and we knew some of the same people. He told me there were numerous people actively working to get Crystal help. I didn't email him back. Even though he said he wasn't trying to get more information for the article, he was a reporter and that was his job. I called my minister crying, and I don't do that. There were more stories and TV appearances; a Go Fund Me Account was set up by Ryan

Holets, the police officer who had found her in the alley; and finally a "State of the Union" appearance by Ryan, his wife, and Crystal's adopted baby.

Could I understand a twenty-seven-year-old police officer who saw a suffering young woman and believed he could save her? Absolutely. I had done the same thing when Crystal was sixteen.

I am Lou. I am Crystal's mother and she still calls me Mamma. This is my journey—walking back into the light . . . no more secrets.

CHAPTER 2

MEET CRYSTAL

I met Crystal just before her sixteenth birthday, and she moved in with us shortly after. Although I am Crystal's third mother, I consider her to be my daughter, and I continue to love her deeply. What makes you a mother? The world is full of people who become mothers in ways far beyond giving birth. I became Crystal's mother when she accepted my love and, in turn, gave me her love and trust. We have an unwritten bond, and I made a commitment to Crystal that I have not and will not walk away from.

Crystal was put up for adoption at birth, and her adoptive parents handed her over to me at sixteen. I know bits and pieces of her life before she came to me, but I now realize how little I understood. I already had seven children when Crystal entered the mix. Three were younger and four were older, including my stepdaughter, who was an integral part of our family. I was young, naïve, and believed I could fix almost anything—including a scared and troubled teen!

I was a fixer and thought little was beyond my powers. The only thing I knew I couldn't fix was DEAD, and I would tell my children that if they killed themselves while drinking and

SURRENDER

driving, I would still be angry when I met them in the afterlife. Now grown, they like to remind me that only those in my generation are drinking and driving—they all Uber. I never thought to warn them about heroin; I had no idea it would be the villain. When heroin addiction hit my family, I was ill-equipped to handle the journey that was to come.

This is not Crystal's story. This is my story. But the story would not exist without Crystal.

I wrote the following in 2001 as part of Crystal's college application process. Looking back, I can see how naïve I was! But it seems like a good place to start.

> The first time I saw Crystal, she was curled up next to my godson on the couch in my son's room, hands over her mouth to cover her crooked teeth; she seemed like someone trying to disappear. I thought she had the saddest eyes I'd ever seen. She was scared and confused, and my husband and I agreed to let her stay for a few days while we got some clarification on the situation and her relationship with her parents. From what we were told, she had been living out of the house for months; staying with different friends until it was time to move on. At the time we met, she was staying with my best friend for a couple of weeks. She and my godson were dating, so it was not the perfect situation! While there, Crystal got pretty sick and tried to get her parents to come and pick her up, but they refused. Ultimately they put her belongings in the front yard and told her to come get them. I think Crystal felt totally rejected and lost.
>
> My friend, not knowing how to handle the situation, called CPS and suddenly Crystal was reported as

MEET CRYSTAL

a runaway and the police became involved. The police called Crystal's parents and told them they had a legal responsibility to take care of their minor child. Threatened by police involvement, Crystal's father began calling my friend at all hours and driving up and down their street late at night looking for their daughter, whom he now claimed he wanted at home. Crystal said she was scared to go home because she feared they were going to just lock her up. Crystal ended up at our house because her parents didn't know us or where we lived, and we all wanted to be sure that Crystal was going back to a safe environment. She was scared and uncertain. Her parents had told her that they were going to send her to Happy Hills or some similar group home for troubled children. After spending some time with Crystal, my husband and I agreed to speak to her parents and ask them to let her move in with us. We didn't think she needed anything that a little love and listening couldn't solve, and we believed we were a better alternative than Happy Hills.

    I don't know what makes a couple decide to take in an extra child, especially when they already have seven, but there was something behind Crystal's sad eyes that made me believe she was just a kid who needed a break. While Crystal's relationship with her father had not completely deteriorated, her relationship with her mother seemed completely beyond repair at that point. There was a tremendous amount of anger on both their parts, and Crystal's mother was determined to send her away. Crystal had rejected their extreme involvement in their church; they expected her to attend three to four times a week, along with several other unusual demands. Their lives truly revolved around their religion. This was also a church that encouraged parents to "dish out" tough love to children who rejected the church and its beliefs—such as putting her belongings in the front yard when she would not adhere to their demands.

At first they were totally against the idea of Crystal coming to stay with us. They insisted that she come home. I spoke to an attorney and, realizing we had no rights to have her stay, encouraged her to go home. We left the door open with her father and stayed in touch with Crystal by phone. Her dad had her copy verses out of the Bible and read them out loud to him. About a week later, he called and asked us to meet with him. We met at a restaurant down the street where he handed Crystal over to us along with three boxes of her belongings. He told us that the religious therapist they were working with said that if they were going to cut ties with their daughter, they should do it now. I believe Crystal's father loved her and simply saw our house as a better place for Crystal than Happy Hills, and it was clear that her mother was determined to have her out of the house.

We were a bit taken aback, and Crystal was devastated at how easily she felt they threw her away. I met her father at the bank the next day to have CPS papers signed and notarized that would allow us to deal with schools, doctors, and so on. Crystal came to live with us the first of July, a few months after her sixteenth birthday. We did not hear another word from Crystal's parents until November of that year. At that time her father called

MEET CRYSTAL

to tell me that they had been advised by their church-based counselor to have no further contact with Crystal until she was an adult. Crystal's reaction was to dye her hair purple.

That began Crystal's life with our family, and she has proved to be everything we thought she could be and more. She graduated from high school in the top part of her class and was involved in student council, volleyball, softball, and volunteer activities. She was also elected homecoming queen by her classmates, which I think is a good example of the tremendous strides she made in developing friendships as well as confidence in herself.

Although we have treated Crystal as part of our family, we have always encouraged Crystal to keep an open mind where her parents and brothers were concerned. The first Christmas that Crystal was with us, her brother from Canada came to visit his parents and came to see Crystal. It was a big step for Crystal. After that her father began calling and occasionally stopping by. It took over two years for Crystal to agree to see her mother, and although they have both tried, that relationship remains strained. Crystal's family left Texas shortly after her graduation from high school and moved to Branson, Missouri.

When Crystal graduated from high school, I wrote this for the headmaster to read for graduation. I think it does a pretty good job of describing how I felt—and still feel—about Crystal.

From the moment I saw your face, I was touched with

love and felt you had come to complete my family. What a delight it has been to watch you grow! In the beginning you were quiet and shy... and we were all a bit unsure what to expect from one another. Late night talks, daytime talks, a house full of siblings, sibling talks, family dinners, family trips as we learned, adjusted and grew together... and what has emerged? A beautiful, confident, determined young woman. We are proud of you, Crystal! Do trust yourself. You have a good head on your shoulders and a good sense of what is right for you. Try new things, take risks, cherish your friends, and always know we are here, and we love you.

Seventeen years later I look back with wiser eyes, a humble heart, compassion, and acceptance of my own limitations and expectations. But this is not a story about my entire life or Crystal's entire life. This is a story of addiction—a five-year window of grief and pain and frustration, with heroin playing the leading role. It's a story that changed me, brought me to my knees, ripped my heart out, and took me to a place of anger I didn't know I was capable of. And like all good stories, the ending is still unknown.

I grew up with addiction. My father was an alcoholic, my uncle and grandfather were alcoholics, my sister, Linda, leaned more toward marijuana, LSD, and hallucinogens—it was the sixties! When I was a freshman in college, I went to stay with my sister in Austin and lay awake all night listening to a seventeen-year-old boy scream while my sister and her well-meaning friends tried to get him off heroin. I remember my sister telling me, "Heroin is a drug for stupid people; never touch it." This was

MEET CRYSTAL

coming from a woman who regularly dropped acid to keep herself "even." We were twenty-one months apart in age, very close and as different as two people could be. I lost her to suicide when we were twenty-four and twenty-five. Crystal reminded me of Linda in so many ways. Maybe I thought I could save Crystal when I couldn't save my sister. I thought my life experiences of addiction and suicide made me well equipped to take on the challenges of this child. I knew she had addiction problems going in, but I don't think I had any idea what that really meant.

It was 1998 when Crystal moved in and became part of our family. My older kids were twenty-one, twenty, nineteen, and eighteen, and my younger ones were twelve, eleven, and nine. The older kids were off to college, so Crystal became the oldest at home. Emma, my twelve-year-old, came home from summer camp to find she was sharing a room! I let the girls redecorate the room and make it their own. We had a celebration dinner and welcomed Crystal into our lives.

We all tried our best. We kept Crystal at Dallas Academy where she was already attending school. They knew her better than we did, and we felt that their backup support would be essential in the coming months as we got to know each other. We immediately put her in braces to correct the crooked teeth situation. From the moment I first saw Crystal, she kept her hand over her mouth when she talked and was visibly embarrassed by her teeth. She told me her parents would dangle braces as a reward. When her grades improved, or she started behaving better, then they would let her have braces. It seemed so cruel.

I was a church person, so I tried to get her to come to church with the family, but she wanted no part of it. Since my husband

SURRENDER

wanted no part of it either, I let it go. I don't know exactly what happened previously with Crystal and church and religion. I knew her dad was a minister when they lived in Canada, and she always spoke happily of her life there, but whatever occurred once they moved to Dallas turned her against the institution in a big way.

I knew she was hurting; she had been given away by the only family she had ever known. She missed her brother who was still in Canada, and she felt like her father, who she really trusted, had thrown her away and chosen her mother. She didn't talk much about it, and I didn't push. I started doing what I did best—I was mom, or to Crystal then and now, Mamma. I went to her sporting events, fixed her meals, told her I loved her and that she was smart and beautiful, helped pick out clothes for dances, and had the "all night" graduation party at our house. Crystal did not have the best reputation at school when she came to live with us, so I spent time with other parents assuring them that our home was a safe place for their children to visit. I believe Crystal knew I loved her and wanted her as part of my family . . . not just for the short term but forever.

Crystal tried her best to fit into the family, but there were always pieces of herself that she held back, parts I could not reach or heal. There would be times over the next twenty years that she would pull away or go inside herself. At times she would try to reject us as her family, and then, just as fast, she would pull us close again. There was a hole in Crystal that I could not fill. The abandonment by her family left a void, similar to, but in some ways worse than, a death. Her parents were still walking the earth, occasionally reaching out . . . only to hurt her again. It was a connection she could not completely sever, and a part

MEET CRYSTAL

of her longed for their love, acceptance, and approval. It was an impossible situation that always ended in shame and judgment for Crystal.

In 2013, Crystal was twenty-nine and living in Santa Fe. She had graduated from the College of Santa Fe and decided to remain there. She had gone through a few relationships, some better than others, multiple jobs, some better than others, but a few years before she had landed in a good relationship with someone she loved, and it appeared they were building a life together. We had met Jim on multiple occasions, and he and Crystal had been at my son's wedding in 2009. They seemed happy.

In March of 2013, I was surprised when I got my first call from Jim telling me that Crystal was doing heroin and he was fearful for her life. The problem had been going on for a while at that point, but I don't know exactly when they started using. I know they started using together. Jim tried to explain it to me, but I'll never know if the version I got was the true one: He told me they had a very sick friend who was dying, and it all started with sharing his opioid pain killers. Moving on to heroin was a predictable scenario.

I would guess that Crystal took to heroin immediately; addiction was already in her genes. I've always felt that Jim was much more addicted to Crystal than to drugs, but he willingly went along for the ride. I don't know the timing; it could have been weeks or months, but Jim told me that he came home one day and Crystal had a needle in her arm. She then put the needle in his arm. The "high" was faster, cheaper, and easier!

Over the years, Crystal told me on multiple occasions that she was better at being a heroin addict than at almost anything she had ever tried in her life. She had no fear of needles, and she never got squeamish shooting up herself or anyone else. She knew how to find the vein, be it the arm, leg, foot, or neck. And as her addiction progressed, she carried Narcan to pop people back in case of an overdose. She was a responsible heroin addict. She found a home in the heroin community, where she was respected and admired for her skills. She was a natural.

At first Crystal and Jim bought small quantities of heroin for their personal use, then larger amounts as their habit progressed. It didn't take long for Crystal to decide that it made more sense economically for them to buy a larger quantity and then sell it. That business strategy only works if you sell the extra. Less and less was sold and more and more entered their veins. Crystal did not come home for the holidays that year. She said money was tight, and I sensed that she and Jim were fighting. They were supposedly both working, but they never had any money. In retrospect, I think things were spiraling fast.

When Jim called me in 2013, he said he was clean. He had gone to California to stay with his sister for an extended period to kick the drugs. Crystal told me he was in California because they needed a break from each other. I could tell, in our limited conversations, that she was angry with Jim, but I just chalked it up to relationship problems. When he returned to Santa Fe, Crystal's drug use had escalated and she was doing meth as well as heroin. I think Jim thought he could handle Crystal and her addiction, but he soon became scared that her life was in danger, and that's when he reached out to me.

And so began the multiple calls and mixed signals. Jim would call and tell me that Crystal was on the brink of dying, and I would call Crystal and she would sound fine. That was before I knew how totally normal a heroin addict can sound when they are high. She

MEET CRYSTAL

would tell me that Jim was overreacting and I should stop worrying. Then Jim would call back and say it was all good and I didn't need to come. This went on for a couple of weeks.

I talked to my other kids and told them Crystal was using heroin. They were stunned. Heroin was not on our radar. They wanted me to go to Santa Fe and intervene. I went back and forth on what to do. I knew lots of people in recovery; mostly AA, and they told me it was a fool's errand if a person didn't want help. Crystal was making it very clear that she did not want or need my help, and she certainly did not want me coming to Santa Fe.

Finally, Jim's calls were too urgent for me to ignore. I decided, that, if nothing else, I needed to look Crystal in the eyes and tell her I loved her and that she was worth saving. I told the kids I was going to Santa Fe, that I would be fine . . . I would take a knife! My oldest son, Jordan, said he would go with me. He was thirty-six years old at that point. He was twenty-one when Crystal moved in, so they weren't close, but he was willing to go, and I was relieved. I was marching into unknown territory, and I knew I was not equipped. I had never done any drugs beyond marijuana; I married at twenty-three and had three children by the time I was twenty-seven. If this trip proved nothing else, it proved how innocent and inexperienced I was. Bringing along a 6'2", tattoo-covered attorney seemed like a good move.

CHAPTER 3

INTERVENTION ROAD TRIP

On Saturday, April 20, 2013, I picked up Jordan at his loft near downtown Dallas, and we headed for Santa Fe. Jordan drove. I don't think the two of us had ever taken a car trip of any real length together. It was great! Despite where we were going and what we were going to do, the road trip itself was fun. We talked about so many things, and then one of us would suddenly say, "I can't believe were doing this!" We had no idea what to expect. A couple of the kids had written letters of support for me to give to Crystal, and I had pulled together a group of pictures showing her healthy and happy—a volleyball picture, one when she was homecoming queen, and a couple with the family.

The drive from Dallas to Santa Fe is beautiful, especially the closer you get to New Mexico. There's one section where billboards start popping up advertising what is clearly the most amazing souvenir store ever. There was one billboard after another exalting the array of goods we could purchase at what we had come to believe was "the greatest store on the earth." It was unbelievable! They truly had everything we could imagine: turquoise jewelry, dolls, knives, fudge, moccasins, paintings, snakes, rugs, handmade ponchos . . . the list went on and on. We couldn't wait—plus we needed gas.

And then we saw it: a giant hut-like structure on the side of the road. We were suspicious, but it delivered on every billboard promise. I didn't think I would ever get Jordan out of that place, but we were on a mission. We finally agreed to stop on the way back and spend all the time we wanted, but that would never happen. Our heads were simply in a different place on the way home.

We arrived in Santa Fe late in the afternoon, went straight to Crystal's house, and banged on the door. No one answered, so I called Jim and he met us at a Burger King down the street to give us a key. Jim said Crystal and a group of her friends had been up all night doing drugs and she was probably sleeping it off. I had no idea how to interact with Jim at that point. I was grateful for the call but unclear as to their relationship. I knew that he had been researching detox options and had found a place in Taos that was willing to take her. That was something. I was sick to my stomach, want-to-throw-up-nervous at that point.

We banged on the door again, and when there was no answer, we let ourselves in. It was dark, the blinds were all pulled down, there were syringes on the floor and a belt hanging from the door knob. I remember Jordan saying, "This is a shooting den." It was dirty, with dishes in the sink and junk lying around everywhere. There was a pile of brown stuff on the kitchen table, and I asked Jordan if that was heroin . . . I'd never seen any. Jordan laughed and told me it was a moldy muffin!

The house seemed empty, but then we found Crystal lying on a mat on the floor in the back bedroom. She looked thin and small. I knelt beside my child and shook her until she opened her eyes. She just looked at me for a minute and then said, "I knew you'd come." I asked to look at her arms, and she pulled up her sleeve to reveal the needle marks. Her veins looked bad and she looked terrible. We talked, but I honestly have no real memory of what I said. It was all so unreal. I showed her the pictures and the letters I had brought from home. I'm not sure she comprehended much, and I was probably throwing too much too fast at her—I usually do. Looking at Crystal, so small and broken, I forgot my fear and anger and just fell in love with her again, just as I had fallen in love with her when she was sixteen. I wanted to save her.

Here is one of the letters I gave her, written by her older sister:

Dear Crystal,

I very much hope that you have a chance to read this letter. I am so sorry that I cannot be there in person with Mom and Jordan today to offer you my support.

Crystal, please know how very much I love you, and how important you are to all of us. Although we do not see each other nearly as often as I would like, I think of you as my sister and I love you with all my heart. There is nothing I would not do for you. I hope you know that you can always come to me, at any time, for any reason. I want you in my life, now and forever, and that is never, ever, going to change. You complete our family. We love you, we need you, and our lives would be empty without you in them.

And so, I say all of this with nothing but immense love for you in my heart.

I have learned that you are regularly shooting up

SURRENDER

heroin and using crystal meth. I cannot adequately express in words how concerned I am for you.

    I know I don't have to tell you how serious a heroin addiction is, but I am going to share my concerns with you anyway. From what I understand, you are presently headed down a path from which you may not recover. I am very afraid that your addiction will lead to your death or imprisonment. And I cannot bear the thought of this.

    Crystal, you are such a bright light in the world. You have so much love and so many gifts to share with the people in your life, and with the people you are destined to meet in the future. You are a beautiful human being, and your life is just beginning. I know you've had a hard start, and you may feel terribly tired and worn out at times, but the truth is, we are both very young. We have so many good years ahead of us, so many good memories yet to be made. You have an amazing future ahead of you, filled with joy and love.

    Today, your addiction is keeping you from that future, and it is isolating you from the people who love you most. But I know you are stronger than this addiction. Fight it, Crystal. Fight the addiction and come back to the people who love you. We are waiting here for you with open arms, and we will welcome you back as soon as you are ready.

    Please listen to Mom and Jordan today. Please take them up on their offer to take you to a safe detox environment and rehab. Crystal, you must get clean before it is too late. You will not have to do this alone. We are your family. We love you and we will be here to support you. I promise.

INTERVENTION ROAD TRIP

    Please promise me that you will check in to rehab and get clean. Your situation is extremely serious, and I am worried to death for you. There is a beautiful life waiting for you on the other side of this darkness, filled with people who love you and support you. Please come back to us.
    I love you so much!

I stepped out of the room while Jordan talked to Crystal. He wanted to speak to her alone, and I needed a break anyway. I was simply overwhelmed. I'll never know exactly what Jordan said to Crystal, but I suspect it was some tough talk. I sat down in a wooden chair at the kitchen table; the chair was green. I stared at the rotten muffin and tried to take it all in. I heard a noise and realized that someone was in the other bedroom. A strange man emerged, and I told him to get his stuff and get out. About the same time, Jordan and Crystal walked in. When the guy saw Jordan, he started packing.
    At that immediate moment of confrontation, Crystal was open to going to detox. Jim had researched facilities before we arrived, and he believed the detox in Taos was her best chance. He felt strongly that we needed to get her out of Santa Fe and away from the problems and people there. I had the number for the facility in Taos. Jim had been in touch with them, and they knew who Crystal was. There was a bed available, but Crystal was required to call the facility herself and do the initial intake on the phone. They wanted to know that she was coming willingly and was not being forced. She went into the bedroom and made the call.
    Crystal agreed to come back to the hotel for the night. She

SURRENDER

crawled in bed and went to sleep. She was exhausted and freezing. Jim and Jordan went to get some food, and I stayed to keep watch over my child. I kept covering her with blankets, and she kept shaking. I was shocked at her appearance. I don't think she weighed ninety-two pounds. She was dirty—it looked like she hadn't washed her hair in weeks, but it was hard to know for sure since she kept a knitted beany pulled down over her head. In the light there was so much more to see than in the dark of the room where I had initially found her.

She had started to develop sores on her skin that Jim said had more to do with using meth than heroin. I thought the marks on her arms were scary, but nothing prepared me for her paw-like feet and hands and the marks on her neck. Crystal had been shooting between her toes and her fingers and they were swollen and red, and I guess when those veins were no longer usable, she had gone for the veins in her neck.

Jim and Jordan came back to the hotel, and we sat outside with the door cracked and talked. They ate, but I had no stomach for food. As I finally took a moment to listen to their conversation, I started getting a better grasp of the situation. It was clear that Jim loved Crystal and wanted to do whatever he could to get her clean, but there was no way he was going to get it done on his own. Jordan and I would not be going home the next day as planned. We would be there until we got her into detox. There really was no other choice.

As part of my newfound education, I have learned that you don't walk into a detox facility because you need it or because you finally hit rock bottom and decide you are ready to get clean. Without a whole lot of money, there are steps . . . lots of steps! Beds and facilities are limited, and there are a lot more addicts than beds. Jim had taken the first steps when he contacted the clinic in Taos, gave them a heads-up, and found out they would most likely have a bed. This particular facility was small, only about ten beds, I think. Crystal had taken the next step when she agreed to call them herself the day before. Now the crazy would begin. I don't know how an addict gets themselves into detox without help. One minute Crystal was ready to go, and the next minute she had a million reasons to stay.

Now that Crystal had done the intake interview and they were willing to give her a bed, we needed to prove she was indigent to qualify for the state detox program. Detox and rehab are not cheap. If I keep saying that, it's because that's reality! For most parents trying to get their kid clean, the costs of placing them in a rehabilitation facility are prohibitive. We live in America, and rehab is big business. I'm sure that with $100,000, I would have discovered multiple beds available in multiple locations. I did not have that kind of money.

I had the money to pay the basic intake fees, which were a couple of hundred dollars, and for the medical exam and medications, which ended up running another six hundred or so. I did not have the tens of thousands of dollars to pay for a full program, and Crystal did not have insurance. State aid was our only route. It was Sunday, and nothing was open, but for a hundred dollars we found a remote notary that would come to the hotel on a Sunday morning and notarize a statement from Jim that he had been supporting Crystal for the last two months since she lost her job.

Much to my relief, Crystal slept the first night. I woke up multiple times, pulled the blankets over her and made sure she was okay, but mostly we slept. We were both exhausted. The next morning, the reality of her situation became more apparent. She was jittery and clinging to Jim. I was amazed at how quickly Crystal's withdrawal symptoms were unfolding. I believe she popped some Xanax to take the edge off, but she was still willing to go to detox.

She needed a medical exam, proof of a TB test, and several prescriptions filled before she could check in to the seven-day detox. Seven days—that's all they were offering. A small window to get through the worst of the detox with the hope that she would then be able to qualify for another longer rehab program. One step at a time, and detox was first. They did not do intakes on Sunday, but we never would have gotten everything together in time anyway.

I found an Urgent Care walk-in clinic in Santa Fe that was open. Crystal and I headed there to get her required medical exam. It was very posh for an urgent care center. Nicely dressed tourists with minor ailments lined the waiting room. We stood out for sure. I had still not been able to convince Crystal to shower or remove her beany. Instead, she pulled it down even tighter over her hair. The doctor was professional, if not thrown off a bit by her appearance. In his report, he stated that he had observed track marks on her arms, ankles, feet, hands, and neck. He also noted abscesses and cellulitis. Her pregnancy test was negative, so I guess there was some good news. He looked at the list of prescribed drugs for detox and wrote the prescriptions. We wanted to get on the road as quickly as possible and decided to wait and fill the prescriptions once we got to Taos, but convincing Crystal to leave Santa Fe proved to be a struggle.

Crystal and I met Jim and Jordan back at the house to gather some clothes and pack up necessities to head to Taos. Jim had agreed to move the rest of her things out of the house and deal with the landlord, the cleaning, etc. By this time, Jordan and I realized that we needed Jim as much as Jim needed us.

Once Crystal got back to the house, she had one excuse after the next as to why she couldn't leave. She had pawned the last of her jewelry and really wanted to get it back. Jordan and I left her with Jim and went to the pawn shop, but it was Sunday, so it was closed. I looked at the pawn shop receipt; she had gotten eighteen dollars for the last of her jewelry—eighteen more dollars to get high. I told her I would give Jim money to get it later. I lied.

Then there was her cat. She believed her cat was magical and just could not leave him. To be fair, he was an exceptionally cool-looking cat, and Crystal had always liked cats. She sat in the kitchen petting her cat while I tried to put some clothes together to leave. Jordan was getting frustrated. He took off to get some cash so we could pay off her drug dealer. Crystal had begun selling drugs to support her habit and owed money to a drug dealer in Albuquerque. That had to be dealt with since we didn't want him coming after Jim. Drug dealers don't play! The guy settled for some money and an iPhone that we hid for him to pick up behind the house.

While Jordan was gone, Crystal called some friends to take her cat. They showed up with their kids. They seemed normal to me, but Jim was irritated and said these were people she used with. Heroin addicts with children . . . the new norm. She gave them the cat and they slipped her drugs. She went into the bathroom and came out happier and much more cooperative. Jordan came back, looked at Crystal and then me and said, "I leave for fifteen minutes, and you let her get high?" Fail!

SURRENDER

Truthfully, though, I had talked to the detox nurses in Taos who assured me that we were not equipped to get her clean or deal with her withdrawal. They told me just to get her there. Crystal finally agreed to go if Jim came too, so the four of us got in the car and headed to Taos. Fortunately, it was a beautiful drive and Crystal was happily high. We arrived in Taos, filled the prescriptions, and checked into a hotel nearby the rehab facility. It was close to 6:00 p.m., and it had been a long day. Jordan and Jim shared a room, and Crystal and I shared a room. Crystal really wanted to stay with Jim. I was not interested.

As much as Jim wanted to help Crystal, he was as codependent as anyone I had ever seen, and his primary addiction was Crystal. Years later, he told me that when he returned from California, clean, Crystal had convinced him to let her shoot him up. She almost killed him. Jim's decision-making could not be trusted where Crystal was concerned.

Jordan needed a break and headed to town to get a drink and some food. I ordered some dinner for the three of us and a bottle of wine for me, but Crystal and Jim were more interested in going to soak in the hotel hot tub than eating. At least she would be able to wash off some of the smell. Another reason not to use public hot tubs—I'm not sure there was enough chlorine in the world to make that one clean again! I also believe she must have scored at the hotel. She had a knack for sniffing it out. When they returned, she was very upbeat and not interested in sleep.

Jim went to bed, so it was just me and Crystal. I remember her standing in front of the full-length mirror and saying, "I don't think I look that bad." My response was, "You look like shit!" She laughed. Crystal decided she wanted to paint her toenails, so she proceeded to sit down on the bathroom floor with a bottle of nail polish. I was so tired; I tried to stay awake but kept dozing off. I would sleep for a brief time and then wake suddenly, remember where I was, and rush into the bathroom to make sure she was still there. She was always there, sitting on the floor in the same place, painting her toenails again and again.

We woke up on Monday with a mission. We had to be at the detox facility by 2:00 p.m. or they wouldn't take her that day, and we still had the problem of getting a negative TB test. It takes 48 to 72 hours after administering a TB test to get a reading, and we didn't have 48 to 72 hours. We were all really stressed out. Check out was at 11:00 a.m., but the guy at the desk said we could stay until 1:00. I told him we might need to stay another night, but we were really trying to get her checked in that day. At that point our mission was clear to everyone, including the hotel staff. We weren't exactly trying to hide why we were there or what we were doing. Crystal was starting to get anxious, and I was afraid that in another twenty-four hours, she would change her mind.

Crystal remembered that she had taken a TB test when she started her last job a few months before. We got on the phone and tried calling her employer. The clock was ticking, and HIPPA was not making it easy. They finally agreed to send the test if we could send them a medical release form. At one point, I was walking through the hotel lobby with a glass of wine in one hand and a cigarette in the other. It was noonish. The manager asked me how it was going. I held up my cigarette and wine and said, "About this good!"

It then occurred to me that I didn't have any of the basic items Crystal would need once she got to the facility. It was not a hotel—they didn't supply shampoo, towels, etc. I headed to the Walgreens down the street. All I could find was a couple of brightly colored beach towels. I grabbed the towels, a couple of magazines, and some other essentials and headed back to the hotel. We were running out of time.

When I got back to the hotel, Jordan was packing up. After a lot of faxing back and forth, the TB test had finally arrived at the hotel. None of us had eaten, but we were racing toward a deadline. We loaded up. Jordan was driving like a maniac, but he got us to the facility by 1:45. Crystal popped a handful of Xanax she had in her bag, and we walked inside. Jordan took off to a nearby Wendy's to pick up some food. Jim and I sat down. Crystal sat in my lap. I put my arms around her and just held her. By age, she was a woman. But at that moment, she was a broken child—my child.

We waited for a while. Jordan came back with the food and we ate. Even Crystal ate, but who can resist a Frosty and a cheeseburger? Finally, a nurse walked out, looked at Crystal, and said, "So you're Crystal. You're a mess." They took her phone, she said her good-byes, and then walked into detox. It was hard not to break down as the doors closed behind her. The three of us got in the car and headed back to Santa Fe to drop Jim off. There was not a lot of talk. Jordan and I were ready to get on the road and head back to Dallas.

I was relieved and sad and probably still in complete shock. Relieved she was in detox, saddened by the turn her life had taken, and in disbelief over all that I had seen in the past three days. I thought we had done well. Crystal had taken the first step, and I truly believed we would beat the odds—after all, I am a fixer.

After dropping Jim off, the drive home was quiet and reflective. Billboards advertising the amazing roadside souvenir shop started to appear, but the menagerie of items just didn't hold the same appeal as we headed home. Jordan let me drive.

As we drove across the New Mexico desert, the wind picked up and we could see something dark heading our way. It was so strange . . . something I'd never witnessed. I had seen plenty of thunderstorms coming toward me across a lake or a beach, contours of rain moving in a visible line until it overtook you, but I never found that scary. This was scary. As the blackness consumed us and all light disappeared, the winds picked up and the car started shaking. We were in the middle of a sandstorm. It was so bizarre. We couldn't see anything, and every few minutes a tumbleweed would slam into the windshield. I was driving, and we were afraid if we pulled over, another car or truck would hit us. Finally we were able to position ourselves behind an eighteen-wheeler. We turned on our lights, since that seemed to be the acceptable thing to do, and slowly moved with the line of cars until the storm passed over us. Light re-emerged and we watched the storm continue its move across the desert like a giant black wall. Light to dark; dark to light.

We were anxious to get home so we were planning to drive straight through, but by early morning we decided to stop and sleep for a bit. We stopped in some tiny town with three motels on the side of the road. We tried the first two that looked decent, but they were full. The last one had one room with two beds and we took it. It was really sleazy, but we needed to sleep. The next morning, we threw on our clothes and headed home. The bath was too dirty for showering. Jordan swore he would never stay in a sleazy roadside motel with me again.

CHAPTER 4

FROM DETOX TO DALLAS

I was not allowed to talk to Crystal while she was in detox, but I could call and check on her as often as I wanted. I did call, sometimes two and three times a day. There was nothing I could do but remind her that I was there and pulling for her. It was a small facility, so often when I called the nurse would tell me that Crystal was sitting next to her looking at the clock, counting the minutes until they could administer the next dose of meds to help her through her withdrawal. I would hear her say, "Hi, Mamma." Day two and three were the worst, and she really tried to bail. The nurse told Crystal that she was one of the lucky ones. She had family who cared and were checking on her. Most of their patients were simply dropped off at the door or found their way there alone.

I knew the withdrawal would be painful. I had read about what to expect: tremors, itching, vomiting, diarrhea, insomnia, and so much more. Plus I had no idea what assortment of drugs Crystal was on at that point. I knew she was doing heroin, meth, and Xanax for sure, but I didn't know what else was in the mix. I had gone through detox with my dad as an alcoholic. Alcohol withdrawal can kill you. From what I read, heroin withdrawal would not kill you—you would just wish you were dead!

At one point the nurse called, which surprised me. I was out showing houses to a client. I told my client what was going on and that I had to take the call. He was great. No judging or questions; he just waited while I took the call. The nurse wanted to understand more about Crystal. She told me Crystal wasn't just an addict doing drugs; consciously or unconsciously, she felt that Crystal was trying to kill herself with the quantity and mix of drugs she had ingested.

I tried to walk her through Crystal's history; the adoption at birth and then being given to me at sixteen. I tried to explain the gaping and painful holes that I had never been able to fill. This nurse genuinely cared and wanted to understand how to help. That's one of the gifts Crystal has continued to sustain. When people meet Crystal, they want to help . . . they want to save her. It was a lengthy conversation. My client waited patiently.

Towards the end of detox, they let me speak with Crystal on the phone. I knew she had been talking to Jim as well. The staff was recommending that Crystal go to a two- to three-month rehab and then a sober living house for an unspecified amount of time. I continued to quietly suggest that Crystal and Jim go their separate ways until they both had more time to adjust to their individual sobriety, but they weren't listening. Crystal was looking at places in New Mexico for rehab since she qualified for state aid there. The place she wanted to go was called Hoy, but they did not have any beds available and she needed to complete more paperwork. On April 29, 2013, they discharged a semi-detoxed Crystal to Jim's care.

I have her detox summary papers. They suggested a follow-up

appointment with the urgent care doctor that Crystal refused to make. They then listed Santa Fe Recovery Center as a thirty-day treatment option and Hoy for a thirty- to ninety-day residential program. They had set up a phone screening at Hoy for May 16 at 1:30 p.m. Crystal flat-out refused to go to Santa Fe Recovery Center, and I was adamant that she should not stay in Santa Fe. After a few days, it was agreed that she would come to Dallas and stay with me until she could get into Hoy.

Crystal is not a fan of flying even under the best of circumstances, so it took a few days for Jim to get her on a plane. She was also not thrilled about coming to Dallas, a city she had never taken to. But I think even Jim had to agree that Santa Fe, after only seven days of sobriety, was a considerable risk! It would just be too easy to fall back into the same surroundings, friends, and habits. We leased a storage unit, and Jim helped her move her belongings there. She packed a small bag of clothes and came to Dallas.

It was an interesting time. After the financial crisis of 2008 and a divorce in 2009, I had pretty much lost everything. I had sold my house and was living at the Village Apartments in a 1,230-square-foot space with two bedrooms and a sunroom. My then-twenty-three-year-old son was living with me while he looked for a job, along with my beloved Poe—an eighty-pound white boxer. We were using the sunroom as a dining room. To prepare for Crystal's arrival, I moved the dining chairs to the garage, took down the table, removed the legs and turned the table top into a headboard for Crystal's bed. We put up some curtains, added a space for clothes, and provided Crystal with a somewhat private bedroom space.

Crystal's sister Emma flew down from New York to help ease

the transition. I knew it would be easier to get Crystal on a plane knowing Emma was there. Emma was four years younger, and they had shared a room from the time Crystal moved in with us at sixteen until she went to college. It was familiar territory, and they had always been close.

Emma was also coming to stay so I could leave for a few days. I was turning sixty on May 6 and had planned to go away for three nights with a friend to my favorite beach. I knew I could not leave Crystal by herself so soon after her arrival. I had been saving and planning the trip for a long time, and my kids didn't want me to miss it.

Emma and I went to Love Field Airport to pick Crystal up. I could tell she was nervous and relieved to see Emma there. She did not look substantially better than when I left her in Taos. I think she might have even been thinner than when I checked her into detox, but her eyes were clear and she was clean. Looking back, I think it was more than I should have dumped on Emma. She was only twenty-seven . . . too young to take on a heroin addict. Crystal had some Xanax that we were supposed to monitor and dole out in prescribed dosages. Emma took on that duty. Crystal's birthday was on May 4, the day I left. She was turning thirty-one. I gave the girls some money to have dinner, and Crystal got a new tattoo. I don't think Emma ever left her side for those four days.

I came back on May 7, Emma went back to New York, and Crystal and I settled in to living together. I had been through enough Al-Anon and AA with my father and other family members to know the mantras and the drill. I tried to get her to go to meetings, but she was not interested. I think she was just hanging on, twenty-four hours at a time, fighting through the continuing withdrawal until she could get into Hoy. We worked jigsaw puzzles, I gave her pens and paper to draw with, I placed copies of the serenity prayer around the apartment, and gave her a copy of my dad's AA book to read if she wanted. We talked.

I told her she had fucked up and made some truly bad choices, but it wasn't the end of the world. The important thing was to acknowledge her mistakes, own them, and be honest. Having recently lost the bulk of my money, which was substantial, I understood the guilt and shame of feeling as though you had let everyone down. I was embarrassed to be living in an apartment after having a big house with a pool and all that went with that. I wanted Crystal to understand that this blip of heroin addiction did not need to define her. She had a full life ahead, and she had forgiveness and acceptance from those who loved her.

Crystal's middle name is Hope, and we talked about calling her Hope instead of Crystal to signify a new beginning. For Mother's Day she made me a card out of a piece of notebook paper and a brown paper bag. It said, "If only all mothers were as special as you," and she wrote me a note that said "Dearest Lou or Mamma, thank you so much for your wisdom . . . Grace . . . Love. You have once again saved me—love Hope!" She included a little white ceramic elephant with it. The elephant's trunk is up! That card still sits on my shelf as a reminder of that time and our love.

I was working two jobs, so I could not be there all day to babysit. I told Crystal I was not her warden and would not monitor her every move. I gave her keys to the extra car and arranged for her to do some work at a charity thrift store I was involved with that benefited the terminally ill. I made a donation, and the owner used the money to pay Crystal so she would have some cash of her own. She walked my dog, and my friend paid

SURRENDER

her to walk her dog. I wanted her to stay busy and not feel like a prisoner.

Her appetite picked up, but she still could not sleep. I would wake up during the night and Crystal would be gone. She said she was hanging out at all-night coffee shops, journaling, drawing, and just being around people. I suspected she was also hanging out at bars. Only recently, Jim told me that she had called him from a bar one night to pay her tab since she didn't want me to know she was drinking. It almost seems ludicrous now to reflect on the level of enabling that was still going on between those two.

She called Hoy Recovery on May 16 and did the phone intake interview. They didn't have a bed and said to stay in touch and they would let us know when a space opened. It turned out that detox had not filed her paperwork with Hoy when she left, so we had to start over again from square one. It was frustrating. I would try calling detox and they wouldn't talk to me. Then Crystal would call. We finally got connected with Di Ana who took control of Crystal's case; she was great, and it helped to have a point person. Crystal was dying to get out of Dallas and back to New Mexico.

Crystal had a friend in New York who she said was sober. He volunteered to buy her a ticket to come and visit. Crystal was ready—anything to get out of Dallas for a few days. I had no idea who this person was, but bottom line, Crystal was thirty-one years old. If she was determined to go to New York, I wasn't in a position to stop her. She knew she had to be sober and pass a drug test to enter Hoy, but we had no idea when they would call. The decision for Crystal to stay clean never rested in my hands—only hers.

As soon as she made plans to go to New York, Di Ana called. She gave her an arrival intake date of May 28 at noon. Crystal started telling Di Ana that she had a trip planned to New York and asked if she could come a few days later. Di Ana had no sympathy. She told Crystal she was getting two-hundred-dollar-a-day rehab for free and to get herself on a plane. Crystal still wanted to go to New York, if only for a day, so I bought her a ticket from New York to Albuquerque and left it in God's hands.

We had a couple of days before she left for New York, which was good, since she needed another medical exam for clearance into Hoy. I took her to the Urgent Care Center near me. We waited. The form was titled Residential Treatment Medical Clearance. The nurse was very young and kind. She asked Crystal if she had an eating disorder. I was a little insulted. Crystal had gained ten pounds since she came to Dallas, and I thought she was looking pretty good, but I suppose that was the type of medical treatment this nurse was accustomed to seeing in our affluent neighborhood. Crystal looked straight into the woman's eyes and said, "No, I shoot heroin in my neck." I thought the nurse was going to faint, but instead she smiled and said, "Well, I'll pray for you, honey." I saw it as a positive sign that Crystal was being honest—albeit brutally honest—about her addiction!

We were much more organized heading to Hoy than we had been when she checked into detox. They sent us three pages of instructions including:

What to Bring
Required Hygiene Items
Clothing Items
Optional Items
Please Do NOT Bring! (these will be confiscated upon admission) Items.

SURRENDER

It felt very similar to sending a child to summer camp. We bought the items, wrote her name on the clothing and other items, and then packed it all up.

I faxed her medical clearance and other forms directly to Hoy, put her on a flight to New York, and hoped she would show up sober at the appointed time.

Crystal checked into Hoy Recovery on May 28, 2013. She passed her screening and was admitted. I was relieved. Jim had picked her up at the airport in Albuquerque and driven her there. Hoy was pretty much out in the middle of nowhere.

As stated in the Hoy Recovery admission materials:

> Hoy Recovery Program, Inc. has been dedicated to healing the community since 1974. When addiction and substance abuse services are approached and provided in a manner that is culturally relevant to our community, the individuals served, as well as their loved ones, come away with an enhanced and strengthened outlook and a new lease on life. We aim to provide these services in an environment that's safe, clinical and trauma-informed while also maintaining a sensitivity and awareness of each individual's lived experiences.
>
> Hoy Recovery Program, Inc. is unlike any other substance abuse treatment center in the state. Truly holistic, we care for the whole client–body, mind and spirit, while maintaining spiritually neutral treatments. Our unique approach leads both our residents and those receiving our outpatient services to take their experiences at our center and transition them into their daily lives, allowing for successful recovery even after they've left. Our

method–a balance of evidence-based, best-practice models for addiction treatment and a traditional healing approach–just makes sense.

Our use of individual and group counseling as well as acupuncture and exercise, which have long been found to be effective in addiction treatment, pair well with traditional Northern New Mexico healing methods with which many of our clients are familiar with, comfortable with, and have grown up with. *Curanderas* (traditional healers) lead our clients through meditation, and a *temazcal*, or sweat lodge, is also an integral part of treatment. At Hoy, we also believe in the healing power of relaxation and restoration, so poetry, art, and gardening are a part of our client's daily lives.

The State of New Mexico had essentially given Crystal a free ride, and I was grateful and hopeful. I felt that this was a perfect environment for her healing. She seemed genuinely excited about the traditional healing methods and sweat lodge. For the first couple of weeks at Hoy, she couldn't talk to me, but we wrote letters; some I still have. I corresponded every few days, and she was pretty good about writing . . . at least in the beginning. She told me she was planning on staying the full ninety days. She seemed happy and talked about playing lots of volleyball, feeding the goats and bunnies, and helping to shear the sheep. They even had a llama. Crystal said it was like camp except for working on her "darkness," as she referred to her addiction and all the trappings that came with it.

I believe Jim went out a few times to see Crystal on family weekends. She never told me about the family weekends, so I never went, but Dallas wasn't right down the street either. I was prepared for her to be at Hoy until the end of August and then was hopeful she would go to a sober living house for women in Albuquerque or some other location. I felt strongly that she needed to be on her own and not with Jim.

I had watched Crystal go through a continuous parade of boyfriends since she moved in with me at sixteen. She had been with Jim the longest, but they had headed down a very dangerous road together that almost killed them both. I also felt that leaving Santa Fe would give her a better chance of staying sober. From what I had seen of Santa Fe, it was a wealthy tourist town supported by a secondary population struggling with heroin and meth addiction.

I don't consider myself all-knowing where addiction is concerned, but I had worked the twelve-step Al-Anon program and been to countless meetings. I knew what "triggers" were, and I believed then—and I believe now—that an addict cannot successfully go back to their same life, same people, and same environment and stay clean. My hope was that Jim and Crystal would go their separate ways, at least for a year or so. Crystal had come into the relationship with addiction issues, but they had taken it to the next level together. I had no doubt that Jim loved Crystal, but I wanted her to learn to stay clean on her own. Crystal was an addict, but Jim, although clean, was addicted to Crystal.

I can't tell you exactly when she left the Hoy Recovery Center. She called one day and said she had been released and was with Jim. I don't know if she had been out for days or weeks. I tried to talk to her about the next step, but she said she was with Jim and that's where she wanted to be. I had no leverage.

For years I thought Hoy had released her. It wasn't until 2017 that Jim told me she had been kicked out for having an illegal cell phone. Over the last five years, there were numerous times I brought up Hoy as an option for her to go back to for recovery, but now I realize she had burnt that bridge and going back probably was never an option.

Jim and Crystal went back to living together in Santa Fe. She seemed happy. I asked her about working her program and attending meetings, but it didn't sound like she was doing that. She said NA meetings were just a place struggling addicts went to hook up and have sex and that certainly was not what she was looking for. I couldn't disagree; I'd never been to an NA meeting. I voiced my concern, but she wasn't listening.

In the end, Crystal and Jim decided the best way to stay clean was to have a baby. Crystal's baby was born the beginning of May 2014, so she must have gotten pregnant almost immediately after leaving Hoy. Crystal didn't tell me she was pregnant until it was well past the point that I could argue with her about it. I was worried; I didn't think she had been sober long enough, and I didn't think her body had recovered sufficiently from the heavy drug use to carry a baby. Every one of my kids voiced the same concerns; some more loudly than others, but it was too late for concerns, and so we all got on board to celebrate the baby who was due in May.

CHAPTER 5

AND A CHILD IS BORN

Crystal and Jim were ecstatically happy to be having a baby. They were reading books, eating healthy, and exercising. They engaged a doula—a bit of a foreign concept for me—and they were hoping for a natural delivery at home with a midwife. Crystal and Jim came home for Christmas that year, and Crystal was round and happy. It was wonderful to see her smile, and I put my concerns in a box and tucked them away. I'm good at that.

My friend Sue and I did an online baby shower since I didn't know anyone in Santa Fe. I knew they needed things . . . everything! We wrote a rhyme; it was a cute invite:

Far Far Away in Santa Fe
A Baby Girl is on the way
So join our party & celebrate
With Crystal Champ and Jimmy Slate
With their family of 2 soon to be 3
We created a baby registry
For Friends & Family to join & share
And show these three how much we care

SURRENDER

With Blessings from friends
And butterfly kisses
We'll welcome with joy
This new Little Misses!

The pregnancy progressed without incident, and I never doubted for a moment that Crystal was staying sober. It was a wonderful window of time with Crystal that I will always be grateful to have shared. She told me multiple times that this was the first time she had been totally sober—no drugs, cigarettes, or alcohol—since she was fourteen.

When Crystal came to live with us, her adoptive parents told me she had learning disabilities that revolved primarily around sequencing. They had enrolled her at Dallas Academy the year before, a school that had a multisensory program for students with learning differences. We kept her there. She had always had problems completing tasks, and I figured it was due to the sequencing issues. Now I realize her drug and alcohol use contributed as well. I'll always carry guilt that I missed those early signs. What seemed like normal teenage behavior was most likely hiding deeper issues. I just didn't see it.

Sober Crystal was different. She was focused, and her plans for the future made sense. She truly wanted to be a responsible parent and take care of her child. She started looking into going back to school to get a degree in nursing or teaching. The plan was for Jim to support them until she graduated, and then she could work while he went back to school to pursue another vocation. Jim was doing construction and was very good, but it was taking a toll on his body, and Crystal didn't think he could do it forever.

AND A CHILD IS BORN

They knew they were having a girl, and Crystal's whole focus was on bringing a healthy baby into the world and being her mother. She wanted to be a better mother than the one who had given her up at birth and a better mother than the one who had given her to me at sixteen.

I'm a worrier, so I was hoping they would change their minds and go with a hospital delivery, but Crystal and Jim were happy with their birthing team and set on a home delivery. Crystal was a known drug addict in Santa Fe, and I don't think she wanted the scrutiny that was likely to come if she delivered in a hospital. She was clean and very sure that she would stay that way, so it was nobody's business.

The baby was a bit late, as babies often are. They called to tell me when she went into labor, but it was going slowly. At some point, Crystal had some heart arrhythmia, so the midwife insisted they go to the hospital. Once at the hospital, despite claims of being clean for months, the staff wanted to run a drug test. The hospital was protecting itself, but I know it upset Crystal and Jim.

I was working at school and waiting for the call that the baby had arrived safely. I don't get service in the building, so every time I saw a call coming in, I would race outside to answer. As the afternoon wore on, Jim called, completely distraught, to tell me that Crystal was not dilating beyond four-and-a-half centimeters and they had just rushed her into surgery to do an emergency C-section. Because of the arrhythmia, they might have been concerned about the strain the labor was putting on her heart. They wouldn't let Jim go with her, and he sounded scared and crushed on the phone. All we could do was wait.

Crystal gave birth to an 8 lb., 5 oz. healthy baby girl on May 9,

SURRENDER

2014, that she named Sage. They sent me pictures from the hospital, and Crystal looked radiant and happy holding her daughter. Crystal and Jim had moved into a cute adobe house before Sage was born. It had two bedrooms, a sweet front porch, and a garden. The nursery was set up, and they were excited to be parents.

I will never know exactly when Crystal started using again, but I have always suspected that they gave her opiates after her C-section, and she was never completely clean again. I doubt I will ever really know the answer to that question.

Jim's mom, Barbara, is retired and was able to go to Santa Fe after the baby was born and help for the first few weeks. Crystal and I talked often. She was tired and stressed like all new mothers. There were days when she was grateful to have Jim's mom there and days when it drove her crazy. The C-section healed more slowly than she wanted and there was extra pain with the incision, but she and Jim appeared to be handling everything.

Emma and I drove out when Sage was a couple of months old. I could tell Crystal was struggling a bit. She didn't have a solid circle of friends who were mothers to give her support, and Jim was working a lot of hours. Nothing feels lonelier than being a first-time mother. She needed females to talk to. It's the same for every new mother. There is so much excitement and attention while you are pregnant, and then you get home and this little person needs you nonstop. Emma and I went to Target and bought a bouncy-rocking chair and a few other items we hoped would help soothe Sage. We stayed a couple of days, and then I had to get back to work.

From the time Sage was born, Crystal and I texted or talked every couple of days. She sent me tons of pictures and we tried

AND A CHILD IS BORN

to FaceTime as often as we could. I loved being a grandma and Crystal loved dressing Sage up and sending pictures. By August, she was working for a veterinarian part-time and getting ready to start back to school. She was engaged with the entire family and texting back and forth about Jordan's engagement and my daughter-in-law's pregnancy.

I went back out to Santa Fe in mid-October by myself, and we had a nice visit. We drove up into the mountains where the aspens were changing colors, and we took a long walk with Sage. The leaves were stunning, and I have great pictures of that day. Crystal seemed better and more adjusted. She was taking walks every day with Sage around the park and loved how people interacted with her daughter. She was a proud mamma! Crystal had found a couple of friends with kids by this time and seemed to be settling into motherhood. She spoke lovingly about her child and their future.

I asked Crystal how the whole sober thing was going. She was completely comfortable talking about it, and I felt like she understood her line. She told me that Jim could have an occasional drink, but she knew she could have nothing. Crystal's addiction relapses had always begun with alcohol and then progressed. She seemed to get that now and even made jokes about it. We all went out for a steak dinner, but Sage wasn't thrilled. We spent the dinner with one or the other of us bouncing the baby while the others ate, but it was still fun.

Crystal came over to my hotel in the morning to let Jim sleep. We played with Sage on the bed and watched TV. Sober Crystal thought a lot more about money. She didn't feel like their little house was turning out to be the best fit for a baby and wanted to go look at some apartments where the floors were carpeted so Sage could crawl and move around easier. She was hoping to spend less money on rent so they could save. We found a nice complex that had reasonable rents, a washer and dryer, a pool, and a hot tub. Crystal wanted Jim to have a place to soak his body so it wouldn't hurt all the time. Jim's mom was spending a good amount of time in Santa Fe helping with Sage, so she also wanted a room where Barbara could stay to avoid the expense of a hotel.

I thought it was a great idea. It was clean and still close to school and Jim's dad. It seemed like a lot less work with a new baby than the older adobe house with no dishwasher and a yard. She broached it with Jim, but he didn't seem nearly as interested in a big apartment complex as Crystal. I think he liked living more on the fringes.

On October 27, 2014, Crystal sent me the following text. (James and Ann Burnett are the parents who adopted Crystal at birth and gave her to me.)

> So the Burnetts are coming to see Sage ... James's work sends him somewhere annually ... and he chose abq and booked tickets before asking me. And then made it clear it was about Sage and that Ann was really upset that I hadn't told them. All this info was given to me backwards
> And at first I was OK about it ... but the more I think about it its starting to bother me ... I just don't know if I want my daughter thinking they are her grandparents ... even though I guess technically they are. I just don't know if I can have a relationship with them
> Even though they basically invited themselves here for

AND A CHILD IS BORN

like over a week and have no boundaries because they consider her their granddaughter
My therapist at rehab told me I have to deal with this ... so I guess I should start the process ... but I'm already feeling anxious and uncomfortable about it.

Crystal was still wrestling with this relationship and had not told them about the pregnancy. After Sage was born, I think Crystal told her brother, and he told their parents. Crystal had done a lot of work on boundary setting while she was at Hoy, but she was aware that she had more to do. She agreed to let them come. It wasn't for a few months yet, and we spent time talking about how to set boundaries when they came and what role she wanted them to play in Sage's life. James and Ann were emotional bombs in Crystal's life that could blow at any moment. Whenever they came into the picture, Crystal always had setbacks.

They had contacted me while Crystal was at Hoy, and it had not gone well. I had not communicated with them since that time. Fair or not, I believed that these two were as toxic to Crystal as the drugs.

For example, on July 3, 2013, Ann sent me the following email while Crystal was in rehab:

How is Crystal doing? Is she still in rehab? I'm assuming you have opportunity to visit with her from time to time?
China has decided we are too old to continue giving us the certificate we need to work in their country. So we are moving back, it appears, to Edmonton.
We are trying to figure out our itinerary for this summer, and how to go around and collect our "stuff." Can

you please get from her [Crystal] a list of what we have in Santa Fe? Does she have any ideas of how we can get it to Dallas to pick it up?

Thanks!

Ann

Rereading my response, it was probably harsher than it should have been at the time, but I felt they were always more concerned about their belongings than about Crystal, and I couldn't imagine how or why they would think she could deal, from rehab, with getting their belongings to Dallas. I was still raw from the whole heroin road trip rescue mission. I should have done better, though. Crystal was their daughter too.

July 7, 2013

Hi Ann,

Sorry not to respond sooner, but I've been trying to figure out how to even respond to this email.

When I went to Santa Fe to get Crystal, she weighed about ninety-two pounds and was probably within a week of dying. After surviving the pain of detox and then thirty days with me, she weighed 120 when I sent her off to rehab. The first thirty days of rehab, she was allowed no contact with anyone. She is now allowed to call on a limited basis on the facility phone and talk for about ten minutes once a week, maybe. She sounds good and seems determined, but her focus today, tomorrow, and for the rest of her life will be to live a clean and sober life. Your "THINGS" are very low on my priority list compared to the life of this child!

AND A CHILD IS BORN

After your father passed away, I did everything I could to dissuade Crystal and Jim from becoming involved with your "THINGS" in any way, shape, or form. Your "THINGS" are not their responsibility, and frankly they are not in a position to deal with them . . . especially now. When I packed Crystal up and we got her out of her house to go to detox, your "THINGS" were at the top of her thoughts, and how to handle them and what to do with them weighed on her. You had apparently called a few weeks before to find out where your "THINGS" were when you heard she was doing drugs. Crystal would never have sold your "THINGS," and if you knew her at all, you would know that. Calls to question where your "THINGS" were seemed to continue while she was with me and your concern about your "THINGS" over HER was a trigger that always had a negative effect. Because of that, I will not, in my limited conversation time with Crystal, bring up this topic.

I can tell you that I think Jim took the furniture pieces out to his parents, and Crystal has a storage unit in Santa Fe which I pay for but have no access to. If you want your "THINGS," then you will have to go to Santa Fe and transport them back to Texas yourself. Jim is not in contact with Crystal right now, and I am the only one who has any access to her. She will be in rehab for at least another thirty to forty-five days and will then be moving to a sober housing facility . . . I hope! It will be her choice, not yours, when and if she decides to get in touch with you.

I am sorry if this sounds harsh, but I have learned that truly "THINGS" don't matter; people do!

SURRENDER

So, I was a bit of a bitch! Looking back on this email, a couple of things stand out. First, that Crystal and Jim were not in contact. That turned out not to be true. Second, that she would be at Hoy for another thirty to forty-five days . . . wrong again, and lastly, that she was planning on moving to a sober housing facility. There was a lot I didn't know!

On October 31, 2014, Crystal sent me pictures of two costume options for Sage to wear for her first Halloween. One was a fairy and the other a lion. Both were precious, but the fairy won. This is the text I sent back:

October 31, 2014
Mom to Crystal
I think you should let her be a lion half the night, so she can roar, and a beautiful princess the other half . . . that sort of exemplifies her personality! Love you, have fun, and be safe.

Crystal and family did not come home for the holidays that year. With school, work, and Sage, she said it was just too hard to travel. She did continue sending me pictures and texted every couple of days. Sage was growing so fast, and I was sad that neither of us had more flexibility to travel. All seemed great.

With so many kids, we do a Christmas drawing every year for gifts. Crystal texted on December 4 to find out who she was buying for and to discuss presents. She told me Sage wanted a xylophone and that the best gift for them was money. I was sad they weren't coming to Dallas, but Jim's dad and wife were in Santa Fe as well, so I knew she would be with family. I tried to remind myself that Crystal now had Jim's family as well as ours and her own. I had to share. Jim's mom lived near Dallas but was still going out to Santa Fe quite often. I think Crystal's love and trust in Barbara was growing, and I was happy she had another strong female figure in her life.

She asked me to send my cheesecake recipe, a family favorite we usually made for Christmas Eve dinner. Crystal really outdid herself on the gifts. She created a custom calendar for me which included multiple photos of everyone in the family as well as individual pictures to mark birthdays. It was quite an undertaking, and I have no idea how she found the time. It was so precious that I had duplicates made for everyone in the family. She also sent a blown-up picture of Jordan and his fiancée that they took in Washington, D.C., when Jordan proposed.

When we spoke on Christmas Day, Crystal was super excited. Jim's dad had given them a substantial amount of money to buy land around Santa Fe and to help with Crystal's school costs. It was very generous, and I was grateful he could give them the kind of money that could add stability to their lives and really make a difference. I was not in that position.

Crystal went back to school on January 21, 2015. James and Ann were there visiting at that time on the long-awaited trip Crystal had so dreaded. She handled it surprisingly well, and I was proud of her. She told them to leave when she was tired and enforced her boundaries better than she had ever done thanks to the therapy she had received at Hoy. Jim not so much—Crystal told me he was much more affected by Ann than she was this time. We joked that Jim had not had the opportunity for the extensive therapy that she had received in rehab to work on his boundaries and defenses.

In February, I started reaching out to plan another trip out to

SURRENDER

Santa Fe. We were still texting every few days, but she was putting me off on coming to visit. They were moving again, and she was overwhelmed with packing. Barbara had driven out to help. I didn't get a picture from March 12 to March 25—which was not that long, but she apologized. Things continued through the spring with FaceTime and pictures and all seemed well, but there was never an appropriate time for me to visit in person. That should have been a red flag.

In May, Crystal, me, Sage, and Jim all have birthdays in one week. I sent gifts and we texted and talked. On May 7, 2015, Crystal asked if I would trade an Amazon gift card for paying her phone bill. I told her I would just pay the phone bill. She and Sage were both sick and running fevers. They just couldn't shake it, and Sage was down for almost a week. It was the end of the school term, and Crystal was scrambling to get everything done. She sounded exhausted and stressed.

At the beginning of June, I had to put my dear dog, Poe, to sleep. It was heartbreaking for all of us, and Crystal was super supportive with numerous texts and tons of pictures to cheer me up. I was getting multiple pictures of the beautiful Sage almost daily. Crystal, Jim, and Sage were all coming to the beach with the whole family in August, and I couldn't wait to see them in person.

On June 29 when I called, the phone was no longer working.

CHAPTER 6

PONTE VEDRA

For the first time since my divorce in 2009, I planned a beach trip for the whole family to a beach in Florida where I had been going since I was a kid. Ponte Vedra held decades of memories for me, and I was super excited to be going back. All eight kids were coming, including Crystal and her family. With spouses and grandchildren, we totaled eighteen. My grandchildren were eleven, four, three, fifteen months (Sage), and nine months. I was intrigued to see how all the grandchildren would interact.

I had found a great house on VRBO that fit us all, a miracle in itself. It had six bedrooms, a den, a huge living space, and a large kitchen table where we could all eat together. It was right on the beach and a short walk to the hotel and clubhouse that had three pools, a restaurant, and work-out facilities. This was my happy place, and I couldn't wait to have everyone together.

I drove with one of my sons and we filled the car with all the necessities. I wanted it to be special and easy for everyone. I packed two pack 'n play cribs, sheets, boogie boards, extra pillows and blankets, beach towels, toys, and books. I had never stayed at this house, so I didn't really know what to expect.

Crystal's trip planning should have been my first clue that things were a bit off. Crystal did not want to fly directly from New Mexico, which made no sense to me. She and Jim drove with Sage to Dallas, a long drive with a baby, and then flew from there. She said it would give them a chance to see Barbara, and she wanted to bring her stroller and a few other things to put in my car to have at the beach. In the end, she didn't bring the stroller.

Crystal also wanted to rent a car at the airport and drive to Ponte Vedra. It was important to her to pay for the rental. It was about a forty-five-minute drive from the airport to the house, and we were trying to have multiple folks driving together. Crystal and Jim did not have a credit card that was acceptable to rent a car. Emma ended up putting it on her card, but Crystal insisted on paying her cash.

Emma and my oldest daughter, Angie, arrived about the same time as Crystal, Jim, and Sage, so they all drove together. We couldn't get the house until 4:00 p.m., but my son Mick and I had arrived early and gotten the club membership set up to give us access to the pool and beach until the house was ready. I was grateful that Sage would arrive before the other grandchildren. I wanted to be able to give her and Crystal my undivided attention.

Mick and I were at the pool when they arrived, and I couldn't wait to get my hands on Sage! Mick and I took Sage in the baby pool while the rest of the group changed into their swimsuits. Sage loved the water, and Crystal was such a proud mamma. We had a nice couple of hours with Angie, Emma, Mick, and I doting over Sage while Jim and Crystal watched on happily.

PONTE VEDRA

We took Sage down to the beach. She had no fear of the ocean and just kept stomping in the waves laughing. A water baby for sure!

Almost everyone else converged on the house at 4:00 p.m. Only the Denver crew was getting in late. I had not realized they were all arriving so early. From previous vacations, I liked getting to the house early, going to the grocery store, and getting the beds and rooms ready. I was such a control freak about that stuff—note I said "was." My children made fun of me and reminded me that they were grown and could make their own beds and go to the grocery store as well. My only job was to relax and play with my grandchildren.

It was wonderful! They did the shopping, took turns cooking, and I truly sat and appreciated it. We played on the beach, built sandcastles, swam, ate meals together, caught up, and just enjoyed each other. I had brought glycerin and bubble mix to make giant bubbles, and at night we had dance parties with the kids . . . they were hysterical to watch. At night, after the kids were down, my grown children would send me to bed and head to the beach to party and play night frisbee as well as plenty of other shenanigans I don't want to know about. There is nothing in life that makes me happier than seeing my grown children and their significant others having fun together.

There were obvious signs at the beach that, in retrospect, we all should have picked up on. As a family, we had moved on from Crystal's heroin addiction and time in rehab. No one was bringing it up or making it an issue, but I can now see that it was still very fresh for Jim and Crystal. We weren't offering any judgment, but they felt it anyway. On some weird level, Jim felt like we blamed him for her heroin addiction. It wasn't true, but

SURRENDER

I'm not sure he's gotten past it to this day. We were just there to enjoy our vacation, and we weren't looking for problems.

Crystal was trying to pay her way and pull her weight at every turn. She went to the store and bought a bunch of sunscreen and water. I could tell Jim wasn't happy, and she went and returned it. He told me years later that she heard one of her siblings saying that she shouldn't be spending money she didn't have, and it hurt her. However, I never wanted anyone spending money they didn't have on our vacation.

We've continued this annual beach trip; this will be our fourth year. I am fortunate to have exceptional children, but they are exceptional in diverse ways, and some simply make a lot more money than others. The ones who make money have always been very generous in contributing to the trip, and the ones who cannot contribute financially give in an assortment of equally important ways. Nobody expected Crystal to be paying for things at that point.

Crystal and Jim were also disappearing for prolonged periods of time with Sage, but I just figured they were on their own schedule. Sage wasn't sleeping great, and I think she was up some at night, but Crystal also stayed up late into the night, not with Sage, but working a jigsaw puzzle. It was Jim who got up early with Sage while Crystal slept in. There were also times they left Sage with me, which was fine, and went for long walks or drives. There was obvious tension there, but I honestly didn't think much about it. I was so sure she wasn't using. I now know that was a ridiculous assumption, and I just did not want to see it.

It was only after we were home and things had gone south that I learned she was partying on the beach at night with everyone, smoking marijuana and drinking. My daughter-in-law had gotten up one night with her nine-month-old and found Crystal in the living room trying to shut some doors to the patio. She said her behavior was very strange. She couldn't get the doors to lock and was pushing heavy wooden furniture up against them to secure the house.

I don't think anyone felt like it was their place to confront Crystal or judge what she was doing. This was the first time we had all been together in years, and everyone was just focused on catching up and having fun. I don't know what I would have done if they had come to me. I thought she was on track, and Jim didn't say anything to the contrary.

On Saturday everyone started heading home. The Denver crew left first. Crystal and Jim were flying back to Dallas and then driving on to Santa Fe. I knew I would see them back in Dallas before they left. They were staying a couple of days to visit with Barbara, and I was driving some of their stuff back with me. While at the beach, Jim and Crystal had asked Angie to be Sage's guardian if anything happened to them. She was touched and agreed. Angie later told me that when she hugged Crystal good-bye, she melted in Angie's arms in tears. Another "cry" we missed. Mick and I packed up the car and headed back to Dallas; it was a two-day drive.

Mick and I arrived home on Sunday, August 16, 2015. It was Monday or Tuesday when Crystal came by to get her belongings. I know I was distracted. I had just gotten back in town, my phone was ringing off the hook with work, and I needed to make some money. If I'd known what an important day it would be, I would have been more present, paid more attention, listened more carefully. I hugged Jim, hugged and kissed Sage, and then put my arms around Crystal to pull her close and say good-bye. I

SURRENDER

told her to drive safely and let me know when they were back in Santa Fe. It was a routine good-bye, one I had done a hundred times with my kids over the years. I watched them drive away and waved.

That was the last time I saw Crystal.

CHAPTER 7

RELAPSE—CAN WE TALK ABOUT IT?

Most of my communication with Crystal over the last two-and-a-half years has been by text and occasionally over the phone. This is a record of our text conversations. I have compiled these messages from multiple phone numbers beginning in August 2015. These texts tell the story—or at least they provide the framework in which the story can be told. Most of the texts are between me and Crystal or with me and my children or Jim. I don't consider these text messages from my daughter Crystal. They are the texts of a heroin addict. The texts are sometimes selfish, often manipulative and demanding. Most are sent to get what she needs from me at that moment. They are also occasionally angry and sad, but still I feel that love creeps through.

My text messages are sent by a heroin addict's mother. They are also often angry and irritable, but love creeps through here as well. I list phone numbers for Crystal to show the sheer quantity of phones she went through, phones with numbers long ago lost or stolen. Staying in touch was a challenge. None of these phone numbers are currently operable for Crystal.

There are also text messages from Crystal on a phone

belonging to a guy named Steve and subsequent texts between me and Steve directly. Crystal originally gave me Steve's number to reach her when she did not have a phone. Crystal stayed with him at one point until they had a falling out. Steve did, however, stay in touch with me. During extended periods when I didn't hear from Crystal, I would call Steve, and he would go and look for her. Steve was the first person to call and tell me that Crystal was pregnant again. He had seen her panhandling on the highway.

I wish I had more voice messages to fill in the gaps, but I only have three or four. It's one of the absurdities of how Crystal's addiction had taken over my life. When Crystal called, I answered. I answered when I was in meetings, with clients, asleep—I even stepped out of my daughter's ordination ceremony to take a call. I had no boundaries. If I saw a 505 prefix, I took the call. Every other day I swim a mile and a half, and it takes me about an hour. That was the only time I didn't keep my phone with me. I lived under an umbrella of anxiety that if I didn't pick up the call, I might never hear from her again.

The longer Crystal was using, the less she called. Texting was less personal, and she wasn't really interested in talking to me. She was interested in what she could get from me: a phone, a hotel room, bail. I was part of the world that Crystal had left behind. A world where people worked, lived in houses, took care of their children, and bathed. I think hearing my voice hurt and touched her in vulnerable spots. And I probably preferred text as well at that point. Our conversations were just repeats, shallow exchanges about family. Me asking if she was ready to get clean; Crystal telling me she just couldn't see a way to live life without heroin.

RELAPSE—CAN WE TALK ABOUT IT?

August 21, 2015; 8:15 a.m.
Crystal to Mom
Morning ... by the way we made it home and unlike Jim I got a day to recover ... quick question ... my therapist wants to test me for bi polar what do you think. I was kinda shocked at first but I dunno

Mom to Crystal
I would ask why ... what does she see in your behavior that suggest that. If she has good response then no harm in getting tested. I have only dealt with it from the MANIC end!

Crystal to Mom
It's because of my highs and lows. I thought you'd have insight

Mom to Crystal
It doesn't hurt to get tested. Love you

Crystal to Mom
Thanks love you too

Things went downhill very quickly after Crystal and Jim returned home from the beach. Around August 22 Jim called me, beyond upset. He wanted to know if I had talked to Crystal that day. When I said I hadn't, Jim told me Crystal was gone. He had come home from work and all her stuff and Sage's things were gone, along with the car. He was beside himself. She wasn't answering her phone, and he didn't know where she was. I tried to get more information, but he was

SURRENDER

too upset to give me much. I told him I would text her and try calling.

I don't recall who heard from her first, but when we spoke, she was irritable and thought we were all overreacting. I'm not sure exactly how long she was gone. Jim sent me the text below on August 23, so it wasn't long.

In subsequent conversations between the two of us, Crystal said she needed to get away and her plan was to take Sage to Jim's mom's house where she would be safe.

August 23, 2015; 1:36 a.m.
Jim to Mom
Sage and Crystal are back safe were both going to be working what the next step is

August 23, 2015; 3:55 p.m.
Mom to Crystal and Jim
Please let me know if you need me; I am always here and available . . . I want to respect you as adults and parents to make your own decisions. You guys have a beautiful and special little girl so do all you can to preserve what you have. Love you

When Crystal and I spoke, I asked if she was using again, and she said yes. I asked if she had put a needle back in her arm and she said yes. I told her she needed to go back to detox, and she basically agreed. There was no universe in which I thought Crystal could stop using on her own. I was sad and feeling guilty about not seeing the signs, but Crystal was an addict and I knew relapse was always a possibility. Deep down in "Lou" world, I just hoped

RELAPSE—CAN WE TALK ABOUT IT?

Crystal would be different; she would be the exception to the rule. I went back to the internet. Rule #1: If you are a heroin addict, you are either using, clean, or dead—and Crystal was using again.

I am a big believer in the twelve steps and working the program. You can't get clean by wishing it were so; you must be willing to do the work, and I had never seen Crystal eager to do that. She left rehab, went back to her same life with Jim, and got pregnant. I know as the mother of many . . . children don't keep you sober—they make you want to drink!

I tried to have a conversation with her about sobriety and balance. I had watched Crystal take on one thing after the next as soon as she left Hoy. She kept going faster and faster; she immersed herself in the pregnancy, delivery, and then taking care of Sage. She piled on school and studying, she got a part-time job with a vet, and then there were the simple chores and errands that become part of the nonsense of living. Her primary job should have been to stay clean, but there simply was no time for meetings. Crystal wanted her addiction to be buried in the past, and she wanted to pour herself into what she considered to be a "normal" life. Crystal was running from heroin as fast as she could, but heroin was faster.

While waiting to get into detox, Crystal's addiction progressed quickly. She started disappearing and staying out all night, and Jim started looking to get Sage into daycare. Crystal was talking to Taos and working toward getting back into detox, but in the meantime, she was scoring drugs and staying high. Crystal was trying to do everything we asked, but I think we were the ones in denial. We wanted Crystal fixed, so we launched a rescue plan: send her back through detox, alleviate the pressure at home by helping with childcare and bills, give Crystal the time to take

SURRENDER

care of herself and put this relapse behind "us"—not Crystal, "us." Boom! It was not a fun time for anyone.

In retrospect, I believe we were all trying to control the situation by making decisions for Crystal. We were making the decisions out of love and fear, but I wonder if any of us were really listening to Crystal. Compassionate listening . . . it's something I'm working on. Did any of us truly listen to Crystal's struggles and suffering? Did our attempts to handle the situation just add to her feelings of frustration and failure?

August 24, 2015; 3:37 p.m.
Jim to Mom
Crystal came back this morning haven't spoken to her she's been asleep all day

I have no idea what she did last night it looks like she slept in the car. I am going to Albuquerque tomorrow to see Sage's doctor and pick up medical records once they have that I think she can get into daycare so hopefully this week or next

August 27, 2015; 2:57 p.m.
Mom to Crystal   (505.231.XXXX)
You are my daughter and I am your mother . . . that will never change! I love you and hope you hare having a good day! XXOO

August 29, 2015; 3:45 p.m.
Mom to Crystal   (505.231.XXXX)
How is your day going? When are you seeing the new counselor? I love you

RELAPSE—CAN WE TALK ABOUT IT?

August 29, 2015; 9:38 p.m.
Mom to Crystal   *(505.231.XXXX)*
I love you forever; I love you for always . . . You are my child and I will always love you

August 30, 2015; 1:37 p.m.
Crystal to Mom   *(505.231.XXXX)*
Im fine everyone is stressing way to much I love you

Mom to Crystal
Ok, thanks for letting me know. I am concerned about you. Haven't talked to Jim; is Sage starting school tomorrow?

Crystal to Mom
Yes And I am going to meet this therapist so that's positive.

Mom to Crystal
Great! Let me know how it goes and if you like him

Crystal to Mom
K

August 30, 2015; 5:00 p.m.
Crystal to Mom   *(505.231.XXXX)*
Went really well I am going to do ten sessions

Mom to Crystal
Great! Proud of you for going! Love you

SURRENDER

August 31, 2015; 2:00 p.m.
Mom to Crystal (505.231.XXXX)
How is your day going? Was Sage excited to start school? Are you in class as well? Love you

[Crystal left me a testy voicemail while I was at work.]

August 31, 2105; 3:55 p.m.
Mom to Crystal (505.231.XXXX)
Just got your voice mail. I'm at school so can't use my phone. I simply asked how your day was going. I am concerned but not horribly. Trying to let you work it out but just here if you need me. I'm working and doing my thing. I will be concerned . . . comes with being a mother and a grandmother . . . I have that right.
This is not my first rodeo

September 1, 2105; 12:50 p.m.
Crystal to Mom (505.231.XXXX)
Sage is adjusting well I think she is gonna b great once adjusted

Mom to Crystal
Thanks for letting me know! What are her sizes? I wanted to send her a little something. Also, I don't think I have your current address so can you send?
Love you

RELAPSE—CAN WE TALK ABOUT IT?

September 4, 2015; 5:56 p.m.
Crystal to Mom   *(505.231.XXXX)*
[Text with two pictures; one of sunflowers and the other of shallots in a heart shaped bowl.]
Sunflowers, sage and mint I grew this year.
At least my green thumb is still working

Mom to Crystal
Beautiful!

Crystal to Mom
Oh and Jim's shallots of course

Mom to Crystal
Very nice . . . I can't grow anything

Crystal to Mom
I don't believe that. You just work so much

Mom to Crystal
True that! I am just leaving school now. I love you

Crystal to Mom
I love love love you Mamma. Talk to you tomorrow

Mom to Crystal
Ditto

I can't remember everything that occurred during that two-week period; there were a lot of moving pieces and people. By then, Barbara had driven out to help and Sage was starting daycare. Jim's dad, Barbara, and I had agreed to share the costs of daycare. Jim's dad paid one month, then Barbara and I split the next month, etc.

Crystal was seeing a therapist that Jim's dad had found. Dr. Azra's specialty was dealing with heroin addiction. He was a recovering heroin addict himself and seemed to have a decent success rate. Crystal called me after one of her sessions and said Dr. Azra had talked to her about relapsing. He said it was not unusual for addicts to relapse multiple times. I reminded her that she had been relapsing since she was sixteen with one drug or another.

Jim called me later that day and said he wasn't sure he could handle anymore relapses. Although home, Crystal was disappearing at night to score drugs and was high most of the time. I was sympathetic. After pulling her off the floor the first time, I knew it was unlikely she would get clean until she got to detox, and detox was a week to ten days away. When Crystal was high, she seemed functional, very organized, and sounded normal. It was when she started going through withdrawal that things would get bad. I had no idea how much Crystal was using at that point. I didn't know if she was shooting up to get high or using just enough to keep from going into withdrawal.

September 8, 2015
Crystal to Mom (email)
Hi Mamma,
Let me start by repeating my thanks to you for your help right now. Many negative words, thoughts, and feelings come to mind when I think about this mess I

have created. Yet since I am trying to use my "shield" to filter out negative thoughts, I feel as though I have a long way to go. My gratitude however is overflowing and I am just really sad that I have hurt and worried my family, something I have been meditating on all day. Also, we just had a rough day with Sage and feeling sick. Fortunately, Sage only has an ear infection, poor thing, yet it could be a lot worse, right! So, hopefully for the last time, thank you for helping us and taking a strain off our shoulders. So here we go. Hopefully I will get into Taos by the end of the week and I am continuing to push, push, push to MAKE it happen ... Just like I have watched you do over the years. I love you dearly and am so sorry that I have asked you for financial help."

In "addict talk," when Crystal said she was feeling sick, I recognized that meant she was feeling the effects of withdrawal. I knew she loved Sage and Jim and was trying to get it together, but it was hard. Then she gave me a list of past due bills that she needed me to pay. I kept stressing to her that she had a disease that could be treated, but she was carrying extraordinary guilt and shame, and I didn't have the words left to alleviate her pain. I just kept repeating that I loved her.

September 8th was also the day I made a questionable decision, but it's the kind of decision a heroin addict's mother will make. I started sending money to Jim to buy heroin for Crystal. I didn't believe she could handle going through withdrawal on her own, and I knew she was already getting sick—not just from her email but from talking to her on the phone and from Jim. She got testy with me on a couple of occasions. She thought

SURRENDER

Barbara was spying on her and going through their trash. We were all hovering, and it was driving her nuts. I didn't want Crystal disappearing in the night to buy drugs and possibly not coming back or ending up in jail. I don't think Barbara had any idea what was really going on, and I still thought I could control the situation with my actions.

I told myself that sending money to buy heroin was short term; just until she got to Taos for rehab. I think my kids would have been furious with me had they known . . . secrets. I took on more work at school. Daycare, utility bills, phone bills, money for drugs . . . it was all adding up. The costs of supporting a heroin addict can become overwhelming.

CHAPTER 8

FROM DETOX TO HOMELESS

September 11, 2015; 4:09 p.m.
Crystal to Mom
Hi mom I'm using Jim's phone to send the info so the motel is called the whitmore inn phone #575-737-XXXX…it's around $60-$70 a night… king room was $69 so we were going to ask you to send $140.00 for gas, food and prescriptions… Call if you have any questions.

September 13, 2015; 9:25 p.m.
Crystal to Mom
Just got to Taos and finding the motel now just a heads up and super thankful for your help we love you and I'll call tomorrow

Mom to Crystal
I love you too!! Let me know if there is any problem with the reservation. I am so proud of you. I know this is not easy but I am with you 100%… go kick this!!

SURRENDER

On September 13, Jim and Crystal drove to Taos, and the next day Crystal checked into detox for the second time. Barbara stayed in Santa Fe to help with Sage. I breathed easier, believing she was back on the road to recovery, but I wasn't quite as cocky this time about my ability to fix her addiction. I didn't call Taos detox constantly like I had before. I checked in once or twice, but Jim was her primary contact this time. I reminded myself that the choice to get clean was hers. The week rushed by for me, but I know it felt like an eternity for Crystal. She made it through, though, and I was proud of her.

At the end of seven days, Jim picked Crystal up from detox. We had talked about the next step, but she had no plans to go to a long-term facility again. She wanted to go home. Her first stop was not to see Sage, however—she wanted to reward herself with a new tattoo! Jim's mom went home, leaving Crystal and Jim on their own.

At first we talked on the phone regularly. Crystal was doing some landscape work with a friend who was sober and working the twelve-step program. I thought that was a positive move. She really wanted to make some money of her own and didn't like being dependent on Jim. Asking for money made her feel like she was being monitored all the time. I understood where she was coming from, but I couldn't blame Jim. He had already had one big scare when she took off with Sage. I thought she was still seeing Dr. Azra, but I'm not sure if that was the case. When we talked, I sensed that she was frustrated, but Crystal also understood that she would need to earn Jim's trust again. At that moment, she seemed committed to her family and staying clean.

I don't know exactly what happened with her landscaping friend. Crystal told me in a couple of conversations that this woman was encouraging her to get away from Jim. She expressed concern over their relationship and thought Sage would suffer long term if they stayed together. She was giving Crystal the same advice I had given her the first time she left rehab. It's probably the same advice that anyone in recovery would have given to a newly clean addict.

I wanted Crystal to learn to stand alone in her sobriety before partnering again, but everything had changed and there was no alone. Jim and Crystal had a child to consider. It was clear things were strained, but Crystal knew she was in no shape to take Sage and leave again. Then things blew up between the two women. I don't know exactly what occurred, but I think she found out Crystal was using again and wanted no part of it.

September 26, 2015; 7:27 p.m.
Crystal to Mom   (505.231.65XX)
[she texted me a picture of the fortune in her fortune cookie]
"Life is a series of choices; today yours are good ones."

Mom to Crystal
Perfect!

September 28, 2015; 8:28 p.m.
Crystal to Mom   (505.231.65XX)
I can't talk. Sorry busy day after Sage goes to school

Mom to Crystal
I love you

SURRENDER

October 16, 2015 2:02 p.m.
Crystal to Mom   *(505.231.65XX)*
Busy busy xoxo

    I will never know how quickly Crystal started using again, but I doubt she stayed clean more than a couple of weeks. By the time Jim called me, things were spiraling out of control once more. He seemed embarrassed and scared... frustrated that he could not control the situation. He loved Crystal so much, but Crystal loved heroin. She was staying out all night most nights, and Jim was completely taking care of Sage. Crystal was coming in during the night and taking whatever items of value she could get her hands on to sell and use the money to buy drugs. Jim wasn't sleeping and was trying to handle all the childcare, which meant he couldn't work. He called me completely rattled and said Crystal had come home in the middle of the night and Sage had woken up. Crystal went into her room, but Sage started crying and didn't want her mother to pick her up.
    Daughter or granddaughter? Right or wrong, at that point my primary focus became Sage and her safety. It was clear that Jim needed to get out of Santa Fe with Sage immediately. They were living in an apartment at that point. I never saw it, but Crystal had complained about the nosy neighbors and thin walls. It was certainly not the kind of apartment we had looked at the previous fall when things had seemed so hopeful. I figured the neighbors were noticing her all-night comings and goings, and there had to be some fighting as well. Sage was also at a school that I knew would be required to "report" if they felt like there was a problem with Crystal and Sage was in danger. I was terrified that someone would call CPS and we would never get Sage back.

FROM DETOX TO HOMELESS

On Halloween, Jim dressed Sage up in a costume and took her to her school party. That was Sage's last day at school in Santa Fe. It took time to get Jim to leave Santa Fe. He had Sage and not much help. It was a little confusing to me where his friends and family were. He seemed to be doing everything himself. Despite what Crystal was putting him through, Jim was unselfishly concerned for her. His life was crashing around him, and I can't imagine the scope of feelings raging through his mind, but he hated leaving Crystal. She was his love and the mother of his child.

Jim agreed to leave Crystal with the car; she basically was living out of it at that point. He packed some clean clothes, sweaters, and blankets for her. Winter was coming, and he wanted her to be warm. He also bought her a phone and made sure it was activated and working so we would have a way to stay in touch. They rented two storage units, and Jim helped Crystal move her things. She was angry. She felt like we were taking her home as well as her child. Leaving the car gave her some mobility and a place to sleep, but it was far from adequate shelter. I handled the payment for her storage unit, but I had determined that I would not give her any money directly.

November 2, 2015; 2:56 p.m.
Mom to Jim for Crystal
When you talk to Crystal please remind her that she is homeless, and you and Sage are also homeless because you can't work and take care of Sage fulltime. Especially if she comes in at night and takes everything of value you own. You are coming to Dallas to get a break and regroup so you can figure out what to do next. You have

SURRENDER

tried to talk to her. In the end what you're doing is not working. You can't have a relationship with someone who is using. Crystal needs to decide to be sober if she wants to have a relationship with you or Sage.

Please tell her that I love her but that I cannot be complicit in her addiction!

We offered rehab again and again, and I would continue to offer rehab. Crystal was not interested.

Jim left Santa Fe with Sage and arrived at his mother's house in Texas on November 7, 2015.

CHAPTER 9

HARD CHOICES

The decision to let my daughter live on the streets was one of the toughest decisions I have ever had to make. Jim and I discussed paying the rent for a couple of months, but we agreed that it would only become a flophouse for Crystal and her friends to do drugs. Jim was also on the lease, so there was liability if they destroyed the property.

In the beginning, I justified that this would be a wake-up call for Crystal; she would hit her "rock bottom" and agree to go back to rehab. I'll never know if we made the right decision. I did not know what else to do. I still thought we could make her want to get clean. Pleading, guilt, threats, love . . . I was willing to try anything. I just wanted her to go back to rehab. I didn't get it. Believing I had control of any kind was giving myself way too much credit. It was always Crystal's decision. I had not put the needle in her arm, and I would not be the one to take it out. Addiction is a powerful disease, and there is no magic solution for those who love the addict. Families and friends are left helpless, loving, sleepless, and hanging. It was only going to end when Crystal decided it should end.

SURRENDER

In my head, I knew Crystal's hurtful words and the choices she was making were not coming from the daughter I knew, not that precious girl I had loved and nurtured. My daughter would never steal, lie, walk out on her baby, or choose the streets over those who loved her. This was not my Crystal; this was a heroin addict—but that's not the whole truth either. This was Crystal, but she was no longer a child that I could make excuses for. She was a thirty-three-year-old woman with a child of her own. I may not have liked it, but Crystal was making these choices.

Still I wanted to find a way to make excuses. Crystal had wounds that had never been healed. We all carry emotional damage of one kind or another. If we are lucky, somewhere along the way we do the work to let it go and find a way to reconcile our suffering. Crystal never did that. At fifteen, Crystal was devasted when her parents dumped her belongings in the front yard of their house and told her it was no longer her home; they never wanted to see her again. The damage done was permanent and deep—the kind of abandonment that is not easy to get past. I do believe that Crystal's parents did what they thought was right, but I did not want to repeat that scenario in her life.

I did not close the door. I told Crystal I loved her and was praying she would find the strength to get clean and reclaim her life. I offered rehab again. I felt different than I had in 2013. I knew I couldn't fix this problem for Crystal. I had put her into detox and rehab once and then supported her habit and paid her bills while she got herself into detox the second time. Not being able to fix Crystal's addiction was hard for me to admit, but this time I knew it was up to her. Crystal had chosen to abandon her daughter and live on the streets. She had chosen heroin.

HARD CHOICES

I called and spoke with Crystal's doctor. He couldn't acknowledge that she was his patient, but he was willing to talk to me about heroin addiction in general. I was struggling with my decisions and was looking for some guidance . . . any guidance. He told me that he did not support giving help of any kind to a heroin addict until they were willing to seek treatment.

I spent my evenings, a glass of cheap chardonnay in my hand, cruising the internet and reading blogs and articles by other parents about their struggles, losses, and strategies for coping with an addicted child. At least my child was still alive.

I printed out the Amy Winehouse lyrics to "Rehab." I could hear Crystal loudly shouting, "No, no, no" every time I offered rehab. That was my Crystal!

I found an anonymous poem online called "Take Me in Your Arms."[1] I included a couple of verses below, but it's worth the full read. It was sobering and descriptively real.

So you'll start inhaling me one afternoon,
you'll take me into your arms very soon.
And once I've entered deep down in your veins,
The craving will nearly drive you insane. . . .

And you will return just as I foretold!
I know that you'll give me your body and soul.
You'll give up your morals, your conscience, your heart.
And you will be mine until, "Death Do Us Part"

Yes, I was coping great . . . really on my game! I should have taken myself to an Al-Anon meeting, but I thought I was doing

---

[1] http://www.wowzone.com/heroin.htm.

just fine. I was strong, and I wanted to be there emotionally and physically to help Jim in any way I could.

Jim was in Texas settling into his mother's house with Sage, and I knew it was the last place he wanted to be. He was tired, depressed, and broken. His life had completely blown up. Jim and I were staying in close touch and sharing with each other when we heard from Crystal, although he was hearing from her much more than I was at that point. We talked on the phone and texted, trying to offer each other support. He was planning to go back out to New Mexico before Thanksgiving to deal with transferring the car title to Crystal and take care of the rest of his stuff.

Barbara was adamant about getting the title to the car transferred to Crystal's name. With everything else going on, I didn't understand the urgency, but Barbara was totally right on that one. A couple of months after transferring the title, Crystal wrecked the car. I'm not sure if Crystal or someone else was driving, but they deserted the car at the scene and ran. Assuming drugs were probably part of that equation, the car did not tie back to Jim or his address, which was a relief. I was already getting monthly notices for Crystal's overdue student loans and unpaid credit card debt. Crystal had tied those items to my address, but luckily, I was not a co-signer and just ignored the bills by putting them in my "Crystal" file.

Once the car was gone, she was truly living on the streets!

November 12, 2015; 2:54 p.m.
Mom to Jim
So sorry you and Sage are sick! Please let yourself get well before you think of heading out to Santa Fe. You will need to be rested and well to see and deal with the roller

coaster Crystal is right now! We both need to continue to remind each other that she is not herself . . . this is ADDICT Crystal . . . manipulative, lying, stealing! I love you and Sage. I will look for her resident card when I get home tonight. . . . You need to tell me what else I can do and what you need from me to make things easier

November 13, 2015; 7:38 p.m.
Jim to Mom
Talked to crystal nothing new to report . . . call me if you need to talk

November 14, 2015; 8:59 p.m.
Jim to Mom
She texted me that she was OK

November 16, 2015; 2:55 p.m.
Jim to Mom
I talked to her for just a second I'm probably going to leave in a day or two
Status quo I let her know that I had just spoken to Angie and she asked for Angie's number and Spencer's number so I sent her both

November 19, 2015; 8:20 p.m.
Jim to Mom
Have not heard from Crystal tried calling her a few times sent her a text no response. Still debating whether to take off to New Mexico hopefully be back before Thanksgiving

SURRENDER

November 20, 2015; 10:57 a.m.
Jim to Mom
No word from Crystal please text me if you hear anything

Mom to Jim
I will. I am so sorry. Try not to sit and obsess about Crystal. You are powerless! It is a beautiful day; take Sage outside and enjoy the day as best you can. Like you, I am terrified! But Crystal is in God's hands. Call me if you need to talk

12:54 p.m.
Jim to Mom
Just received a text from Crystal she says that she's fine

Mom to Jim
Thank you for letting me know. Keep me in the loop. Love you

November 21, 2015; 8:16 p.m.
Jim to Mom
Spoke to her briefly status quo

Mom to Jim
Thanks, will you send me the last picture you took of her? I need to see it.

He never sent the picture. I was desperate for images at that point. I wanted to see how bad she looked so I could gauge her condition. I don't know why I thought it would make any difference.

HARD CHOICES

Jim brought Sage to Dallas to see me and the family the day before Thanksgiving. It was the first time I had seen them since their arrival. It was so wonderful to hold that baby girl! Looking at Sage was like looking into Crystal's eyes. Even her little walk was so Crystal. Sage was a gift ... a light in the darkness we were all muddling through.

November 26, 2015; 9:24 p.m.
Mom to Jim
Hope you guys had a nice Thanksgiving! Loved seeing you guys yesterday! Love you

November 27, 2015; 1:53 p.m.
Jim to Mom
It was great seeing everyone and I know Sage had a really good time. Crystal called today telling me that she had broken her phone and said that she was going to work on trying to get another one so who knows when I'll hear from her again

Mom to Jim
Ok, so sorry! Are you still going out to Santa Fe? Hate she does not have a phone but we can only do what we can do. Let me know if I can do anything. Give Sage my love

Jim to Mom
Planning on leaving Sunday morning was going to stop by your house maybe and pick up a copy of Crystal's green card

SURRENDER

November 29, 2015; 9:00 a.m.
Mom to Jim
Hi Jim
I'm leaving a brown envelope on the front porch with Crystals documents, some McDonald's coupons, a note and a coloring book and pens I bought her a while back. Give her my love and I can't wait to see Sage next weekend. Please drive safely. Love

Jim to Mom
Just leaving now
having an incredible hard time leaving Sage

Mom to Jim
I am so sorry! She will miss you but be fine! Get this behind you!! Prayers and love your way

Jim was in Santa Fe for a few days. He saw Crystal, and they went through the storage unit and split up more of their belongings. They found Crystal's passport and birth certificate, and she gave them to Jim to hold for safekeeping. Jim headed back to Dallas, leaving Crystal in Santa Fe with a new phone.

Crystal continued to stay in touch with Jim, texting or calling every few days. Nothing was really changing. She kept saying she was getting a place to stay, but it never seemed to come to fruition. Jim brought Sage to spend time with us on Christmas Eve. We exchanged gifts and had a fun time. Jim brought us Christmas poppers—a tradition in his family—and we had a lot of laughs popping them on Christmas Day!

HARD CHOICES

December 24, 2015; 9:07 p.m.
Jim to Mom
Thank you to everyone Sage and I had a great time she talked about it the whole ride home

Mom to Jim
Loved having you guys . . . she so precious! Have a Merry Christmas and look to all you have to be grateful for!

December 25, 2015; 11:51 a.m.
Mom to Jim
Merry Christmas! I hope you guys are having a wonderful day! Thank you so much for the stocking, throw and Xmas poppers . . . we are having so much fun with the poppers! I will send pictures! Love to you, Sage and your mom

December 25, 2015; 5:20 p.m.
Jim to Mom
Having fun with Sage today She's had a great Christmas thanks to everyone Merry Christmas will see you guys soon

December 25, 2015; 10:33 p.m.
Mom to Jim
Did you hear from Crystal today?

Jim to Mom
I did, unfortunately status quo

SURRENDER

Mom to Jim
Thanks; how does Crystal sound, better?

Jim to Mom
She sounds about the same. She is hopeful that she'll clean up soon. All I can do is hope for the best

January 2, 2016; 8:52 p.m.
Jim to Mom
Spoke to Crystal she says that she's getting a place within the next few days hopefully so will see other than status quo

Mom to Jim
Thank you! Trying not to bug you but really worry every day! Who's sponsoring the place she's going to live? You guys okay? Love you

Jim to Mom
The Burnetts are sponsoring. We are doing well Sage and I send you love

Crystal reached out to the Burnetts, her previous parents, when I would not give her any more money—any port in the storm, I suppose. They were hoping to get her a place through a church connection they had found, but the room did not come without strings. They were asking Crystal to jump through several hoops to get the place. In the end, I don't remember that anything came of it other than maybe a couple of nights in a hotel. They dropped off my radar, and if they were still communicating with Crystal, I was out of that loop.

HARD CHOICES

January 18, 2016; 7:57 p.m.
Jim to Mom
Crystal sent me a text yesterday saying that she would call haven't spoken to her in over a week

January 18, 2016; 9:40 p.m.
Mom to Jim
I'm sorry. I know this is so hard for you. I miss Crystal so much and feel so helpless . . . get Sage feeling better so she can come for swimming! Best we can do is keep her happy and give her the best life this world has to offer and shower her with love and kisses. For Crystal I can only pray

CHAPTER 10

THE NEW NORMAL

In mid–January 2016, Jim and I fell into a comfortable arrangement with Sage. She would come on Saturday mornings for swimming lessons, spend the night, attend Sunday school while I went to church, and then Jim would pick her up after her nap. Most Saturday mornings I would make the hour drive to pick Sage up and Jim would make the drive to collect her on Sunday. What a delight it was to have this child in my life! With all the Crystal darkness we were dealing with, Sage was the light. The only way I felt I could help Crystal was by helping her daughter and Jim. At that point, I was still very hopeful that she would come back to us.

Most of my weekends I now shared with Sage. I had a car seat in my car, a pack-in-play set up in my extra bedroom, diapers, bottles, and toys. It was amazing how fast I fell back into taking care of a little one. We walked around the ponds in my neighborhood and tossed sticks off the bridge. When it was cold we ran around North Park Mall, threw pennies in the fountain, and ate at The Mermaid Café inside Neiman Marcus. I could have a glass of wine and Sage could get an overpriced grilled cheese sandwich with a fruit cup and fries.

SURRENDER

My oldest niece, Amanda, lives in Dallas, and we have always been very close. She and Crystal are the same age and they, coincidently, had children one week apart. Ryan was one week older than Sage, and by mid-February we were spending most of our Saturday nights and Sunday mornings together. Ryan and Sage became the best of friends and loved their time together, and I was delighted to be spending time with Amanda. Ryan was all boy, and Sage was all girl. Ryan would throw a ball as hard as he could, and Sage would sashay over, pick it up and hand it back to him with a polite "thank you."

For Sage, it was all about the clothes. I kept an assortment of princess costumes, swimsuits, and dresses at my house. Sage would usually change outfits four to five times during the evening. She had her own sense of style, just like her mother. I was always amazed at the way Crystal could pull together random clothing items and always look great. Sage would twirl in front of Ryan, showing off her outfit, perplexed when he didn't compliment her. Fortunately, Amanda and I were all over it. Amanda worked at a children's clothing store and was always showing up with something interesting and new for Sage to add to her wardrobe.

On Sundays we would take Sage and Ryan to Sunday school while we went to church. Sage loved climbing up the ridiculous number of steps at the front of our church, greeting everyone, and then walking down the aisle of the sanctuary while the musicians practiced before we headed to her class. She would do this cute little dance down the aisle, waving and saying hi to everyone. People knew her by name. It was nice.

After church, we would go for donuts and coffee. Sage wanted pink glazed and Ryan wanted orange glazed. The two would run up and down in front of the donut store, looking in the window of the shop next door for the big cat. A couple of wet ones would keep them busy cleaning tables while Amanda and I caught up. They looked like twins with their blonde hair and similar coloring. When the weather was nice, we would take them to the playground or the water park. They would giggle over nothing until they fell on the ground. I'd forgotten what it was like to laugh that hard! The routine was good for Sage, and it was good for me.

Jim and I both continued to have off and on texts with Crystal. Nothing was really changing. Jim had bought another phone. I sent him this text at the end of January.

January 26, 2016; 2:51 p.m.
Mom to Jim
I just want to tell you how sorry I am for all of the pain and sorrow that Crystal is putting you through. I hope she reaches out again but I think it is time that you turn her back over to me. You can't keep living under this pressure. I will buy the next phone if we get that chance ... you can't afford to keep doing it. I'm her mother and she is my responsibility.

Jim went back out to Santa Fe at the beginning of February 2016. Crystal had relocated to Albuquerque. He helped her move some of her things from storage to her "new home." She was living under a bridge, but I didn't really understand what that meant until Jim showed me pictures and explained. There is an interior space between the top of the bridge and the lower structure. Crystal and some other homeless companions had set up a sort of makeshift home inside. I had no idea something like that even existed. They had made beds out of blankets and arranged their other belongings within the concrete enclosure. I had always admired Crystal's ability to make any space cozy and fun, but she had taken it to a whole new level this time! Jim offered to put her up at a hotel, but she preferred the bridge home.

When Jim got back to Texas, we had a hard conversation. He felt it was time for him to go to court to get full custody of Sage. I couldn't disagree and said I would support him. From the time Crystal went back on drugs, Jim stated quite firmly that if Crystal got clean he would not keep her from Sage, and I believed him. Jim's mother had kept him from his father for a good portion of his life, and he didn't want to do that to Sage. Unfortunately, it didn't appear that Crystal had any real interest in getting clean. If anything, she seemed to be embracing life on the streets.

We agreed that, for Sage's safety and security, Jim should pursue custody. He had an ongoing fear that Crystal would show up and grab Sage, and he would have no recourse. I felt that was truly an unlikely scenario, but Jim was very paranoid about it. He was convinced that if Crystal showed up at my front door and wanted to take Sage, I would not be able to stop her. Jim obviously did not know me very well. I would never have let Crystal take Sage without Jim's permission. I would have called the police or one of my very large sons who lived nearby. The last thing I wanted was for Sage to have an addict mother bouncing in and out of her life! I knew he was scared and hurting, but I was hurting too.

Jim's paranoia made no rational sense to me. At that point, Crystal was so far off the rails that I had virtually no contact with her. Crystal was running with a group of other homeless addicts, mostly younger than her. They spent their days panhandling near the highway to get just enough money to get high and eat. No jobs, no rent, no responsibilities other than getting high. I knew she missed Sage, but the longer she was on the streets, the less she asked about her daughter. It was a life of addiction, but also a life of freedom with no responsibility or accountability to anyone.

The bridge home didn't last long. Within a couple of weeks, the police came, cleared it out, and Crystal lost most of the last of her belongings.

February 8, 2016; 9:31pm
Mom to Jim
I hope you are having a better day. I thought a lot about our conversation . . . there is nothing easy about this. I do hope that you will move forward with custody and not see Crystal again. You helped her move things from storage to her "new home" and got her a phone . . . don't let her take anymore from you. She has made her choice. The focus now must be on Sage. She is a gift and we will make sure she feels loved and is given every opportunity to grow into a healthy and happy young lady! Love you

CHAPTER 11

JAIL TIME AND PHONES

The first time Crystal was arrested, I was in Denver visiting my son and his family. Crystal wasn't the first kid to call me from jail, but she was the first one I thought would stay there. She was charged with felony possession. Before I could speak with her for more than a minute, I was required to give a credit card to continue the conversation and set up an account at the Bernadillo County Jail. She begged me to post bond so she could make bail. I said no. I didn't have it, I was pretty sure she wouldn't show up for her hearing, and I wanted her in jail to detox. I knew she was starting to hurt, but for the first time in a couple of months, I slept knowing where she was.

February 13, 2016; 6:17 p.m.
Mom to Jim
She just called me but when I told her I couldn't post the money she got angry and hung up on me. I pulled her up on the jail website and called the number. They said the full amount had to be posted in cash. No date scheduled for arraignment. I am pretty haunted by her

mug shot! I will go online tonight and see if her case has been updated.

February 13, 2016
Mom to all the kids and Jim
Crystal is in jail. Jim and I are in contact. If she contacts you no posting bail please

Various Kid Responses:
-Good. Hopefully she doesn't bond out and will be relatively safe there and withdraw. They can give her medical care. That beats being under a bridge around a bunch of drug addicted men. Thank you for letting us know. Try enjoying your weekend

-Best thing that could have happened. I know it isn't easy :(love you and try to relax

-Thanks for letting us know

My first reality check with the penal system in this country was when they released her from jail the next day and simply dumped her back on the street. Relieved I hadn't posted bond, I was furious! It is not easy to leave a begging and detoxing child in jail, but they didn't want to deal with a detoxing heroin addict either—there were just so many in New Mexico. Her phone and backpack disappeared in the process and weren't dumped back on the street with her.

JAIL TIME AND PHONES

February 14, 2016; 3:26 p.m.
Mom to all the kids and Jim
Crystal is out; released on her own recognizance; no fine!

February 16, 2016; 6:33 p.m.
Crystal to Mom (505.309.XXXX)
Hh

February 24, 2016; 9:41 p.m.
Mom to Jim
Don't want to keep bugging you but I need to know if you heard from Crystal. Thanks

Jim to Mom
She texted me on Monday late at night saying that she was going to try and get her phone and her backpack from the police station. She hasn't text or called since then. You are not bugging me at all I wish I had more news for you

February 26, 2016; 9:29 am
Crystal to Mom (505.588.XXXX)
Hi mom ... it's Crystal and this is my number ... I'm busy right now but am going to try calling you in a little while ... hope your well

Mom to Crystal
I am very happy to hear from you and I love you. If I can't answer my phone please try back. In and out of meetings

SURRENDER

February 26, 2016; 9:31 p.m.
Jim to Mom
I called and talked to Crystal for just a moment just to say that we all love her. She got off the phone pretty quick. She mentioned trying to get on Suboxone so I don't know, just hoping for the best

February 27, 2016; 9:32 p.m.
Mom to Crystal (505.588.XXXX)
I love you forever; I love you for always. Mom

February 28, 2016; 1:49 a.m.
Crystal to Mom (505.588.XXXX)
I am trying to get my life together and I did not realize that my stuff in storage is going to be history . . . if there is a chance that you would pay for one 8more Month . . . I thought there were more days in February but I am mistaken . . . I Understand if you can't and I appreciate all the help . . . I am so ashamed. With all my shortcomings

Mom to Crystal
I will. You can get your life together. You are strong . . . believe in yourself!
I love you.

February 29, 2016; 9:39 p.m.
Mom to Crystal (505.588.XXXX)
Your storage is paid until April 2. I love you beautiful girl.

JAIL TIME AND PHONES

March 1, 2016; 10:27 p.m.
Mom to Crystal   *(505.588.XXXX)*
Good night. Be safe.

March 3, 2016
Crystal to Mom   *(505.588.XXXX)*
The UPS Store
 Let me know you got this

Mom to Crystal
Yes I got it. I will send the phone later today or tomorrow

March 4, 2016; 2:55 pm
Mom to Crystal   *(505.588.XXXX)*
I sent the phone today. It will arrive Tuesday or Wednesday. They have your name for pick up. They have a $10.00 pick up fee but I have already paid it. I will confirm with you when it arrives. Still your Mamma.

March 4, 2016; 3:59 p.m.
Crystal to Mom   *(505.588.XXXX)*
Hey ok well you are the nicest lady ever . . .

March 6, 2016; 9:48 p.m.
Mom to Crystal   *(505.588.XXXX)*
I am your mother . . . I love you. Be safe

March 7, 2016; 12:07 a.m.
Crystal to Mom   *(505.588.XXXX)*
Aw

SURRENDER

March 7, 2016; 10:52 p.m.
Crystal to Mom   *(505.588.XXXX)*
Hi mom ... Just wanted to say hi

March 7, 2016; 10:52 p.m.
Mom to Crystal   *(505.588.XXXX)*
Thank you. I love you

March 8, 2016; 2:52 p.m.
Mom to Crystal   *(505.588.XXXX)*
The phone is at the UPS store under your name for pick up. Love you

March 8, 2016; 9:09 p.m.
Jim to Mom
Crystal texted today and said she missed Sage and wants to get her shit together but she's just not sure. I missed a phone call from her trying to call her back but no answer

March 10, 2016; 10:22 a.m.
Mom to Crystal   *(505.588.XXXX)*
Have you picked up the phone? Thinking about you; stay safe

March 12, 2016; 9:54 p.m.
Mom to Crystal   *(469.236.XXXX)*
Hope you now have this phone. Thinking of you Mom

March 13, 2016; 12:25 a.m.
Crystal to Mom   *(469.236.XXXX)*
Hi hi

JAIL TIME AND PHONES

March 14, 2016; 9:25 p.m.
Mom to Crystal   *(469.236.XXXX)*
Hope you are ok, love u

March 15, 2016; 5:20 a.m.
Crystal to Mom   *(469.236.XXXX)*
Yep love you too

March 16, 2016; 10:20 p.m.
Mom to Crystal   *(469.236.XXXX)*
Love to you!

March 19, 2016; 12:41 p.m.
Mom to Crystal   *(469.236.XXXX)*
Hope you are ok; hope you are happy. Don't understand this journey but it is your journey! Love you always . . . mom

CHAPTER 12

TOM AND MORE PHONES

I don't know when Crystal and Tom got together, but when I called on March 25, a male answered the phone. Welcome to the story, Tom.

March 25, 2016; 6:53 a.m.
Mom to Crystal   *(469.236.XXXX)*
I got your message and tried to call back but a guy answered the phone and said you were unavailable to talk to me. I hope you got the message. I love you Mom

Crystal to Mom
Hi yes I did ive been busy call u later
For some reason I try to call tt but my phone wont let me
I love you

Mom to Crystal
Love you too

SURRENDER

Crystal to Mom
Glad to hear it

March 27, 2016; 10:11 a.m.
Mom to Crystal   *(469.236.XXXX)*
Happy Easter! A day of new life and new beginnings. Be well . . . I love you

March 28, 2016; 9:32 p.m.
Mom to Crystal   *(469.236.XXXX)*
I renewed your phone today until the end of April . . . I hope it is still in your possession! I love you

This is a series of texts that began after a conversation where Tom and Crystal asked me to get them a hotel room. Tom wanted to try and help Crystal get off heroin so she could transition to Suboxone. It was a little confusing to me since I thought he was on heroin too, but I guess at that point meth was his drug of choice. Crystal said it was too hard on the streets. I put them in a hotel.

This would be the first of multiple hotel rooms I would book over the coming years. It was not a straightforward process, especially if the person you were booking the room for was often without any ID and looked like hell. Most hotels and motels would not let me book over the phone with a credit card. They wanted to send me a form to fill out, sign and fax back, not email, with a copy of my credit card, front and back, and my driver's license. I never knew why they would not accept an email scan, but they would not. Upon Crystal and Tom's arrival at the hotel, the manager would usually call me to confirm, and once they looked at Crystal and Tom, they would ask me for an additional deposit.

TOM AND MORE PHONES

Booking a hotel for them typically would go like this. I would tell Crystal what time I would be at my office or near a computer so I could deal with the hotel form. Despite my pleas to get the information to me by a certain time, she usually couldn't. Heroin addicts seem to have no connection to time.

On one occasion, I had a photo shoot for Texas Monthly and needed to be at the location at a specific time. Not hearing from Crystal, I made a copy of my credit card, scanned it into my email and headed out for the photo shoot. While driving, Crystal called me with the hotel information and pleaded with me to do it right then. While driving, I called the hotel and had them email me the form. I then forwarded the form from the email in my phone to Emma in New York to fill out and sign along with my scanned credit card information. Emma printed the form, filled it out and signed it, but she couldn't fax it. She scanned and emailed it to my office coordinator who then printed and faxed the information on to the hotel. I sent an email to the woman at my office saying, "Sorry, it takes a village to raise a heroin addict." I always made light of Crystal's situation. I didn't want anyone feeling like they had to feel bad or ask questions.

I arrived at my photo shoot, sat in my car for a moment, and then put on my lipstick and heels. I walked into the photo shoot with a smile on my face and stood on a staircase with twenty or so other agents to have my picture taken. Just another day in my life with a heroin addict.

March 29, 2016; 5:43 p.m.
Mom to Crystal   *(469.236.XXXX)*
I have no idea if you will get this; sending to both numbers ... Freaks me out that it is not private but here we go. I

SURRENDER

appreciate you called. I know the conversation is awkward but it's hard for me when I feel like my conversation is being monitored by Tom. I know he is part of your life right now and I respect that but I don't know him or anything about him and you know it takes me time to trust anyone. That being said, if he is encouraging you to get clean then I appreciate his efforts and I hope that he is good and respectful to you. You know me so you know I spend a lot of time in prayer for your recovery . . . I do believe that you can beat this. Let me know how the suboxone goes. I am glad you are starting the process. I love you, Mom

7:11 p.m.
Crystal to Mom
Tom is an honest person . . .
He truel
Cares

Mom to Crystal
I'm glad for you

March 31, 2016; 9:43 p.m.
Mom to Crystal   (505.267.XXXX)
This is for Crystal. I hope you are moving forward and working towards getting clean. Know that I love you! Mom

April 2, 2016; 12:46 p.m.
Mom to Crystal   (469.236.XXXX)
If you are serious about getting clean, I will pay for a

hotel for 4 nights . . . that will hopefully get you through the worst of the initial detox. I know you want to try and do this on your own and pray you will be successful. I will arrange payment with a hotel directly once you decide when and where . . . keep it economy! I love you

2:32 p.m.
Crystal to Mom
I love you MOM! I am determined and would really appreciate it I have to figure it out but it wont be till later cause I am running errands and have to stop and grab my stuff across town cause im going to stay away from my area of town

Mom to Crystal
Sounds good! Just let me know.

April 2, 2016; 8:48 p.m.
Crystal to Mom   *(469.236.XXXX)*
So its taken me all day to prepare but I was going to suggest tomorrow I will figure it out and call you love c

Mom to Crystal
Sounds good. I will be at church in the morning and home about noon my time. Love you . . . you can do this!

Crystal to Mom
I know

SURRENDER

April 3, 2916; 9:32 p.m.
Mom to Crystal   *(505.886.XXXX)*
How are you doing? Love you

Crystal to Mom
We are well, planning on researching some hotels tonight. Ill get back to you with the options, K?

Mom to Crystal
Sounds good! Crazy work tomorrow so if I don't pick up I will call you back. Love you

April 4, 2016; 5:03 p.m.
Mom to Crystal   *(505.313.XXXX)*
It's mom…Love you and send me the info and I'll set it up to start tomorrow

Crystal to Mom
I need my number

Mom to Crystal
469.236.XXXX

April 5, 2016; 11:10 a.m.
Mom to Crystal   *(469.236.XXXX)*
Hi Crystal,
Please try to get me the hotel information as early today as possible. I will have to fax forms and can only do that from my office. I will be at my office until 2:00 my time. I love you

TOM AND MORE PHONES

Crystal to Mom
whats your price range

Mom to Crystal
Hoping to keep it in the $60 range with taxes etc but haven't checked the market there

Crystal to Mom
Try the Hampton inn on a cheap hotels website or howard johnson

Mom to Crystal
Is there more than one? Street or area? I will need to call the hotel direct. That is the only way they will let me pay.

Crystal to Mom
Around Carlisle and downtown area

Mom to Crystal
Ok, I will let you know once I have something booked

Crystal to Mom
K

Still April 5, 2016; 2:41 p.m.
Mom to Crystal
I am working on it but the manager is out and they can't figure out how to do it! How's the Days Inn on Ellison? Starting today or tomorrow?

SURRENDER

Crystal to Mom
See the price for the week compared to 4 days please

Mom to Crystal
Only $2.00 a day difference. You are booked for 4 nights and can check in at 3:00. Confirmation # is 485-23XX81. Please use this time well to start getting clean. I love you and will send prayers and love your way!

April 5, 2016; 9:26 p.m.
Mom to Crystal (460.236.XXXX)
Did you get checked in? I just realized I didn't give you the address! Address is 51XX Ellison St. NE Albuquerque 87109
Days Inn

Crystal stopped responding to this phone and ended up texting me from a different number. It was getting late. I had to get up early and go to work the next day, which was a concept Crystal no longer related to. At this point, Crystal had no grasp of time. She was truly living in the here and now with no concept of past mistakes or future plans.

April 5, 2016 10:16 p.m.
Mom to Crystal (505.886.XXXX)
I called the hotel and they said you had not checked in. I sent the address and confirmation # to your phone. Do I need to send it to this one.

TOM AND MORE PHONES

Crystal to Mom
Yes. My phone is lost in someone's car and so if you get this you can reach me here at my friends SarAh"s number. my phone is lost Leftin a cArr

Mom to Crystal
Days Inn.51XX Ellison St NE. 505-344-XX55 Confirmation # 485-23XX81 Paid tonight through Friday night. They are expecting you

Crystal called to tell me that I booked the wrong Days Inn and it's too hard for her to get there from her current location. I ended up cancelling the first reservation and rebooking at the Days Inn closer to Crystal, but it was so late that she decided to go the next day. In the end, this hotel kicked them out after one night, and I went through the entire process again to book them at another hotel. Needless to say, Tom did not get Crystal off heroin.

Mom to Crystal
Call me back. Cancelled the other. Let me see if I can book where you are

Crystal to Mom
She needs a copy of your id
It's already so late and I still have to grab my stuff from a mile up the road
If it is too much trouble then I will research SPECIFIC options
My court date is next Thursday

SURRENDER

Mom to Crystal
I just sent the ID. If you want to check in tomorrow then that is up to you. I thought you were checking in at 3:00 today so a bit confused. They should have everything. I am about to call them to confirm so need to know if you want to start today or tomorrow
You are all set for tomorrow. You just need to show ID

Crystal to Mom
They are not helping me very,
The only reason I didn't check in earlier is because I didn't have my phone and wasn't around anyone with a phone
I do have id

Mom to Crystal
Great, all is set and you can check in at 3:00 tomorrow

Crystal to Mom
Thanks Mamma love you

Mom to Crystal
Love you too

April 23, 2016; 1:58 p.m.
Mom to Crystal   *(469.236.XXXX)*
Please call me and let me know you are ok. I've tried to call a number of times. I love you

TOM AND MORE PHONES

April 27, 2016; 10:01 p.m.
Mom to Crystal   *(469.236.XXXX)*
I did not find driver's license info but Jim has a copy of your social security card and passport. Do you want me to forward? Let me know. I love you

Crystal called me at the beginning of May. I was in Denver visiting my son and his family. Crystal, Sage, Jim, and I all have birthdays the first week of May. Crystal told me that she and Tom had figured out a way to get a ride to Dallas, and they were planning to come and see Sage for her birthday. I told Crystal that was not going to happen and that she could not see Sage until she was clean, and certainly not with Tom. She got very defensive and sarcastic with me and said, "Well, that's your opinion." I told her that was reality, and it wasn't going to happen.

She tried to make some points of her own, but I wasn't backing down. In the end, we compromised. I agreed to pay for a hotel in Albuquerque for a couple of days for Crystal's birthday. She dropped the idea of coming to Dallas and I was able to keep tabs on where she was.

May 6, 2016; 2:55 p.m.
Crystal to Mom   *(469.236.XXXX)*
Hi and happy b day xoxo thanks for everything!

Mom to Crystal
I hope you had a good couple of nights in the hotel.
Thanks for the birthday wishes!
Love you

SURRENDER

May 10, 2016; 7:29 p.m.
Crystal to Mom   *(469.236.XXXX)*
Hi mom I am having a hard time without a smartphone plus I need to be able to use the internet and there r cheaper phone plans thru metro pcs. Please think abut it. Love

I couldn't bring myself to respond to this one. I mean, what kind of mother was I to deprive my heroin addict of a smartphone—such sacrifice!

May 21, 2016; 12:16 p.m.
Mom to Crystal   *(469.236.XXXX)*
Love you always! Mom

May 23, 2016; 9:02 p.m.
Mom to Crystal   *(469.236.XXXX)*
You have a hearing for "supplemental nutritional assistance program" on May 25 at 2 p.m. at Santa Fe County ISD. 39 B Plaza La Prensa 87507. Case # 1200XX552 Call 800.283.44XX if you need to reschedule Love you

May 24, 2016; 4:31 p.m.
Crystal to Mom   *(567.401.XXXX)*
Mamma its Crystal, the phone stopped working due to a problem with the charger. This is my text free #

May 28, 2016; 12:01 p.m.
Mom to Crystal   *(469.236.XXXX)*
Let me know if you get this and if I should renew the

phone for another month. Love you
So is the phone no longer workable? I won't update service for another month if it is dead

That was when I started communicating with Crystal through Steve. Steve was a former addict who was in recovery. He was a friend to Crystal and then came to play a role in my life by helping me keep up with her for a number of years. Steve would occasionally take Tom and Crystal to dinner and let them stay in his shop when he was out working. At some point, Tom and Steve had a falling out, but he was always available to me when I couldn't find Crystal; responding to text messages and going to look for her. He would also let her use his phone to check in with me when she didn't have one. He was one of the few sources of consistent information I could get on Crystal during her years on the streets, and that felt invaluable to me.

June 1, 2016; 4:43 p.m.
Crystal to Mom (Steve's phone)
Mom . . . if you could please pay the AT&T bill and let me know on this phone when you've done it so I can switch the phone number to metro pcs . . . right now I can get two lines with two free phones and unlimited talk text and data . . . the phone number must be active though and that is why I need your help. But all I'm asking is that you help with the $30 bill for At&T and the $75 for storage . . . love you

Mom to Crystal
Will do, I will do it as soon as I get home and text you. Love you

SURRENDER

7:35 p.m.
Mom to Crystal
Phone is done.
Storage is done.

June 1, 2016; 8:35 p.m.
Crystal to Mom *(Steve's phone)*
Thank you

June 5, 2016; 7:19 p.m.
Mom to Crystal *(Steve's phone)*
For Crystal. Did you get a phone? What is the number?

Steve to Mom
This is Steve I have not heard from them in three days, from Tom and Crystal

Mom to Steve
Thanks for letting me know! Her Mom . . . I worry

Steve to Mom
I was going to buy them dinner the other night and I checked the usual places and could not find them. let me know when you hear from them

Mom to Steve
Same . . . thank you

June 7, 2016; 12:08 a.m.
Crystal to Mom *(Steve's phone)*

TOM AND MORE PHONES

Hi mom . . . Steve came to find me and I just wanted to let you now that I am alive and well. I've started a care taking position and no phone yet but soon . . . love Crystal

A caretaking position seemed unlikely. I never heard another word about it.

Mom to Crystal   *(Steve's phone)*
Thank you, love you too

June 17, 2016; 6:01 p.m.
Mom to Steve   *(Steve's phone)*
Hi Steve, sorry to bother you but this is the only number I have for info on Crystal. Haven't heard anything from her. Have you seen her? I just want to know that she is ok. Thx

June 19, 2016; 11:03 a.m.
Steve to Mom   *(Steve's phone)*
I have not. Last time they disappeared they were in Santa Fe will ask around today
I am working a lot right now but I'll check every chance I get

Mom to Steve
Thank you

CHAPTER 13

BACK TO JAIL

Crystal and Tom were both arrested on June 18, 2016. Tom was charged with "Possession of a Contraband Substance Methamphetamine and Tampering with Evidence." Crystal was charged with "Possession of Burglary Tools" and "Possession of Contraband Substance Methamphetamine." Crystal also had an outstanding warrant for failing to appear in court on a shoplifting charge.

She called once again and begged me to bail her out, and once again I refused. I was hopeful they would keep her long enough to detox; although I knew at that point it was unlikely. I don't think Crystal could ever grasp that leaving her in jail was my way of showing love. A wonderful thing about the prison system is the access to information. You can monitor the arrest and release dates online in real time. I also got to see another mug shot. She looked tired and thin.

Tom had some property he was able to put up as a bond. He was released on the 21st and posted Crystal's bond on the 22nd. She was about four days into detox, and I couldn't sleep for worrying about her. I remembered how bad it had been when she went through detox the first time. Then she

SURRENDER

had drugs to help, nurses to monitor, and me on the other end of the phone giving encouragement. I knew she was hurting, but another three days would have gotten her over the hump. Another opportunity lost.

June 21, 2016; 7:00 p.m.
Mom to Jim
Talked to Crystal. She is not a happy camper! Checked jail records and Tom is out

June 21, 2016; 8:15 p.m.
Mom to Steve
If you get a minute would you please call me. Crystal is still in jail but I saw Tom got out today. My plan is to leave her there to detox which feels mean but my only option right now. I know you have been there so curious if you have an opinion. FYI, she is trying to get in touch with you in the hopes you will bail her out

Steve to Mom
I will not bail her out

June 21, 2016; 9:14 p.m.
Jim to Mom
I really hate how New Mexico treats felonies like their nothing, it really gets under my skin that he's out. I hope he doesn't find a way to get her out

Mom to Jim
Me too! I don't think she knows he's out. I pulled up his

arrests and he's had 8 arrests since 2005 but this is his first one since 2011; he had 3 that year!

June 22, 2016; 3:13 p.m.
Mom to Jim
She's out. Tom must have posted bail! Another lost opportunity

June 22, 2016; 3:14 p.m.
Mom to Steve
She's out. Tom must have posted for her after he got out

June 23, 2016; 11:00 a.m.
Crystal to Mom   **(505.582.XXXX)**
Hi mom it's Crystal and I wanted to let you know that I am out of jail and this is our phone number

Mom to Crystal
Yes, I saw Tom was released the 21st and saw you bonded out yesterday. Thanks for the phone number. I hoped you would stay long enough to detox but I guess the road to rehab is back in your court. I hope you will consider changes in your life. I love you.

Crystal to Mom
Okay there are still a number B is of steps I have to continue in dealing with the V events I have
Just because I am out of jail doesn't mean I don't have a tough journey ahead. I am well aware of what I need to do to move forward

SURRENDER

Mom to Crystal
I will continue to send positive thoughts and prayers your way

Crystal to Mom
I realize your lack of faith in my abilities but hopefully in the future I will be able to get back what I have lost with you. There are a few different options for rehab...but until I get my court dates set I am working on trying to get up and out of homeless life...

Mom to Crystal
You will never lose me and I will always love you. My hope is that you will find some support in getting clean so you can take back your life. But on the other end, you are a grown woman and choices are yours and yours alone

June 26, 2016; 3:25 p.m.
Mom to Crystal   (505.582.XXXX)
Checking in and hoping you are doing ok... I love you, Mom

Around this time I had one of my favorite conversations with "addict" Crystal. We usually didn't talk much, and our conversations revolved around me asking her if she was trying to get clean and her telling me no. In one of these routine conversations when I asked her about using and getting clean, she got very irritated and responded, "Mom, I'm not drinking or doing meth, I'm just shooting heroin." I felt so much better!

BACK TO JAIL

June 26, 2016; 9:04 p.m.
Steve to Mom   *(Steve's phone)*
Crystal and Tom are staying at my shop tonight while I'm out working

Mom to Steve
Thank you for letting me know

Steve to Mom
Crystal showed me your picture tonight

Mom to Steve
Unfortunately, I think as long as she is with Tom she will never get clean

July 5, 2016 8:23 p.m.
Mom to Crystal   *(505.545.XXXX)*
I need to know if I need to pay your storage. It has to be paid by tomorrow.

July 6, 2016; 8:49 a.m.
Crystal to Mom   *(505.545.XXXX)*
Yes please, and thank you

Mom to Crystal
Ok. Hope you are okay. Love you

July 8, 2016; 4:49 p.m.
Crystal to Mom   *(720.982.XXXX)*
Mom its Crystal could u please set up my phone again

SURRENDER

Mom to Crystal
I thought you lost that phone. Do I need to send a new phone?

Crystal to Mom
I have a phone I just need the number turned on

Mom to Crystal
The same number you had
Who is the provider
You will need to give me more direction

Crystal to Mom
OK let me go to the store although I think that if u can attach the one number to the phone

Mom to Crystal
Ok but you will need to find out how to do it at the store

Crystal to Mom
In the morning I will go

July 11, 2016; 9:44 p.m.
Mom to Steve   *(Steve's phone)*
Have you seen or heard from Crystal? She told me on Friday, via text, that she would get with me Saturday and have heard nothing. Thx

Steve to Mom
I saw her panhandling a couple of days ago They don't

BACK TO JAIL

talk to me much anymore threw Tom out of my place being disrespectful

Mom to Steve
Smart move on your part. She will have to decide to leave him. Thx

Steve to Mom
You can let her know that I'm here for her but I'm not helping Tom anymore

Mom to Steve
Ok, right now I have no contact number

July 21, 2916; 1:56 p.m.
Mom to Steve   (Steve's phone)
If you see Crystal around will you let her know her phone is at the UPS store. If she still doesn't have her ID then she can give them the code word "pick UPS" and they will give it to her

Steve to Mom
Ok Will let her know if I see her

July 26, 2016; 9:42 p.m.
Mom to Crystal   (505.545.XXXX)
Looking for Crystal . . . any info

SURRENDER

July 26, 2016; 10:22 p.m.
Mom to Steve *(Steve's phone)*
Sorry to bother but have you seen or heard anything abut Crystal? She never picked up the phone I sent and she has not contacted me at all which is unusual . . . she usually reaches out and lets me know she's ok. I just want to know she's not dead! Thank you

Steve to Mom
No I have not heard from them I will see if I can find her

Mom to Steve
Thx

July 27, 2016; 9:41 p.m.
Mom to Crystal *(720.982.XXXX)*
Looking for Crystal . . . have you seen her?

July 28, 2016; 9:38 p.m.
Mom to Steve
Figuring you never heard anything on Crystal but thought I would check back. Thx

CHAPTER 14

PONTE VEDRA 2016

On July 30, 2016, my children and their families left their homes in Denver, Sewanee, Philadelphia, New York, and Dallas to travel back to Ponte Vedra for another week at the beach. Everyone was coming—everyone but Crystal. We were grateful at least to have Jim and Sage joining us. Jim and I had developed a good relationship, and we were working well to give Sage as much stability and love as we could.

Jim was Sage's father, and I was grateful every day that he had stepped up to the task of single parenting. The last thing he had wanted to do was leave Santa Fe and move to Dallas, but he had put Sage's needs first and did what he needed to do to keep her safe. That was deserving of respect. Jim's mom was equally amazing. I don't know exactly what she was doing before Jim arrived with Sage, but Barbara put her life on hold to give Jim and Sage the care they needed. I was delighted to pitch in and offer relief when I could. I certainly wasn't making any progress helping Crystal, so being there to support Jim and Barbara with Sage helped me as well.

I put Crystal on the back burner for the week. I had not heard

SURRENDER

from her since July 8th. I had reached out via text to every number I had, including Steve's. I was worried; this was the longest she had ever gone without contacting me. I was freaking out internally, but I refused to ruin our one week together as a family by dwelling on Crystal. It had been almost one year since I'd seen her. It was hard to believe.

Each time Jim walked down the stairs or out to the beach with Sage, we remembered the previous year when Crystal was there . . . her presence, her laughter, her being. The week passed too quickly. Sage was delighted to be with her cousins and was a bit shocked and saddened when she realized we were not going to all live together forever.

We built sandcastles, swam in the ocean and the pool, had dance parties at night, and talked. Everyone tried to include Jim and pitch in with Sage so he could have time to himself. He liked to take long walks on the beach and look for sharks' teeth; one of our favorite beach pastimes. He carried a sadness about him that none of us could fix.

When we returned home, Jim and I went back to our shared weekends, but he started keeping Sage with him at least one weekend a month to do something special. He had grown into his role as a single father and was much more confident than when he first arrived. That was a good thing.

CHAPTER 15

YEAR TWO—STILL HOMELESS

August 7, 2016; 4:13 p.m.
Mom to Jim
Just spoke to the medical examiners office and they have no unidentified females at this point so I think that is good news.

August 8, 2016; 1:09 p.m.
Mom to other kids
Crystal just called me. She finally went to pick up the phone which is now on its way back to Dallas. I told her it had been there 4 weeks and I called the morgue last night after confirming she wasn't in jail. She said I was being overly dramatic. I will send the traveling phone back again!! Everyone loves a heroin addict. She did tell me she loved me and would try to do better.

Various kids' responses
-Wow. Soooo glad she is alive! By "doing better" is there any chance that could mean getting sober and living a real life

SURRENDER

-I am truly grateful she is alive
-So glad to hear. Love to all!
-Phew! I'm glad she's alive and okay(ish) You were definitely Not being overly dramatic! I'm very glad she called! Love you all!

August 18, 2016; 10:16 p.m.
Mom to Crystal   ***(469.520.XXXX)***
Got your message. Sorry late work. I did pay storage. Love you

Crystal to Mom
Love you mom I may be going to Amarillo to get clean but I won't know for a few days

August 19, 2016; 6:37 p.m.
Mom to Crystal   ***(469.520.XXXX)***
Would love to see you get clean. Keep me in the loop. Love you

August 24, 2016; 2:54 p.m.
Jim to Mom
Went to court today and got sole custody of Sage, bittersweet victory but the right thing to do

    I knew Jim was pursuing sole custody and working through the process, but my heart still sank a bit when it was final. It was the right decision, though; Crystal had been gone almost an entire year. I did not discuss Jim's plans with Crystal. She had not asked about Sage in months. Jim was required to post

YEAR TWO—STILL HOMELESS

"Notice" of his intentions in various publications in Santa Fe and Albuquerque as part of the custody suit. He was afraid that she would see the notices and contest his custody. I was pretty sure Crystal wasn't reading any newspapers at that point.

September 4, 2016; 9:50 p.m.
Mom to Crystal   *(469.520.XXXX)*
Crystal should call me or this phone will be deactivated

Crystal to Mom
Ok ok

September 5, 2016; 7:59 a.m.
Crystal to Mom   *(469.520.XXXX)*
Hi mom its crystal and I will call u in a bit after breakfast I have been busy with all this getting my shit together and I need this number active and sorry ive been distant

Mom to Crystal
I just need to know you have the phone and not someone else since it has been answered by random people

Crystal to Mom
Yes I have it but it is used by my friends sorry for

Mom to Crystal
I am not trying to force you to call but needed to know that your phone had not been stolen . . . I hope you are okay and do love you

SURRENDER

Crystal to Mom
I know and im sorry I love u too Mamma

Mom to Crystal
Tried to call back. My phone didn't even ring! Going out in a few! Love you

September 5, 2016
Mom to Jim and Emma
I heard from Crystal via text. I believe it is her. No real information. I sent a text last night that I was going to disconnect the phone if she didn't get in touch . . . worked. She just said she was trying to figure things out and really needed the phone. I assured her I would keep the phone active as long as I know it is in her possession and that I loved her. Got the "sorry ,love you Mamma" back.

September 6, 2016; 1:28 p.m.
Jim to Mom
I called yesterday and today no answer

October 12, 2016; 7:13 p.m.
Mom to Crystal   *(505-577-36XX)*
If this is Crystal's phone, call me

October 27, 2016; 12:33 a.m.
Crystal to Mom   *(505-639-XXXX)*
3 hi Mamma, it's Crystal and I am alive. Tired and pretty much a totally ashamed, very confused daughter, mother, girlfriend, addict . . . I think about calling. And then my

YEAR TWO—STILL HOMELESS

phone gets stolen . . . along with every other belonging I have on earth. I wander through this city and time passes ever so quickly while I do stop and visualize my life with Sage . . . Tom . . . healthy and successful and as I attempt to get off this drug that has me cursed I am wishing I was on the other side of the life I have willingly subjected myself to . . . dragging with me every miserable compromise I have agreed with . . . every selfish act, crime, and less than honorable attempt at surviving such an insane existence . . . and time passes and I have had so many chances to prove that I am worthy of a better life . . . I want to want and crave sobriety . . . another chance . . . it is so hard. This is my friends phone jake . . . I will tra calling u tomorrow . . . I love u . . . Cryst

October 27, 2016; 7:15 a.m.
Mom to Crystal   (505-639-XXXX)
I am so happy to hear from you and that you are alive! I love you very much and so pray that you can find a way out of this life. Sobriety is your only choice. I miss you in my life and worry. You are stronger than you think and I know you can do this. Know you are loved and I will help you. Mom

This text broke my heart. I could feel "my" Crystal in the words; I could sense her suffering and her struggle. I knew a part of her was craving sobriety. I offered to help again, but then she dropped off the radar and I didn't hear from her again directly until December. I did exchange a series of weird texts with Tom at the beginning of November that at least confirmed she was alive.

SURRENDER

November 7, 2016; 3:58 p.m.
Mom to whoever has the phone!   *(505.639.XXXX)*
Have you seen Crystal?

I never knew who would answer this phone, but I quickly realized I was texting with Tom. He had a style of his own.

Tom to Mom
Who the is

Mom to Tom
Her mother
Who is this

Tom to Mom
I seen her this morning ?did she give you this number to get a hold of her at ?

Mom to Tom
She texted me a week or so ago from this number

Tom to Mom
This is Tom I'll give her the message when I see her. Is it important?

Mom to Tom
No

Tom to Mom
Oh okay I'll ever text you when I see her or call you

YEAR TWO—STILL HOMELESS

November 23, 2016; 10:46 a.m.
Mom to ?   *(505.639.XXXX)*
Have you seen Crystal? This is her mom

December 1, 2016; 9:48 p.m.
Mom to ?   *(505.639.XXXX)*
Looking for Crystal

December 10, 2016; 12:21 p.m.
Mom to ?   *(505.639.XXXX)*
Have you seen Crystal?

December 13, 2016; 3:34 p.m.
Crystal to Mom   *(505.336.XXXX)*
Hey Mamma its crystal and im alive and still in Albuquerque . . . this number is our text free number . . . so it only works around wifi . . . but you can reach me on this number
I love you :-) :-)

December 14, 2016; 7:24 a.m.
Mom to Crystal   *(505.336.XXXX)*
Glad to have a way to contact you and glad you are okay. I love you very much! Please stay in touch.

December 14, 2016; 2:40 p.m.
Crystal to Mom   *(505.336.XXXX)*
I love you mo

SURRENDER

December 15, 2016; 4:15 p.m.
Mom to Crystal (505.336.XXXX)
Love you very much and think about you always. Praying you will find the will to get clean! XXO

December 17, 2016; 4:59 p.m.
Crystal to Mom (505.336.XXXX)
Hi mom . . . r u around to chat while I am on wifi?

Mom to Crystal
Yes

Crystal to Mom
Ok let me see how it works :-)
Im g
Going to try and call

We had a short conversation, but there was not much to say. Things in her world stayed the same, and she didn't want to talk much about it. Every time I tried to get specifics about her life, she would get defensive. I asked her once if she was still with Tom after not hearing from her for a while, and she came back angrily with, "Why?" I replied, "Crystal, I'm just trying to make conversation." Sometimes they stayed at friend's houses, and other times they camped out in the park.

My feelings about Tom were all over the place. I knew nothing about him beyond his rap sheet that I went through when they were arrested together. It looked like he had been at this life a lot longer than Crystal. I had spoken to him a few times on the phone and honestly couldn't understand much of what he said. Crystal told me on more than one occasion that she had tried to leave Tom because he wanted them to get clean and she wasn't ready. I remember her saying, "Mom, I just can't see a way."

Another time she said Tom was really mad that she wouldn't get "clean for him." She almost laughed on the phone when she told me what she had said to him: "I can't get clean for my daughter, or Jim, or my mom or my siblings . . . you are way down the list of people I can't get clean for." That pretty much said it all, but knowing he had some interest in getting them clean made me not hate him.

I lived in a constant state of fear when Crystal was homeless and living on the streets, but I knew my fears were nothing compared to the reality that Crystal was living through. I guess knowing she was with Tom gave me hope that she would be safer.

We spoke around Christmas, and Crystal said they had stayed with friends. All along I had been expecting her to call and ask me to put her and Tom up in a hotel.

CHAPTER 16

NO WIN

January 12, 2017; 1:24 p.m.
Crystal to Mom   *(505.203.XXXX)*
5056887206 the MSID # is 5054104571 and 268435457811399195..is the serial number to the phone I have . . . oh yeah it's crystal and I love you

Mom to Crystal
Who is the carrier? My computer crashed and have a new one going in tomorrow so will be then. Love u too

Crystal to Mom
U can use your phone to activate it. I think it is a virgin mobile.

January 13, 2017; 9:53 a.m.
Mom to Crystal   *(505.203.XXXX)*
I will work on it later today! 2 jobs and I can't use my phone at school

SURRENDER

January 14, 2017; 2:54 p.m.
Mom to Crystal (505.203.XXXX)
That is not the code I need to activate the phone. I need the ESN, MEID or IMEI/MEID number. It can be 11,14,15 or 18 characters, all numbers or a combination of letters & numbers. It can be found on the device packaging, the back of the device or behind the battery. I have to have that number to do anything. Love you

Crystal to Mom
OK cool thanks for your help with this

January 24, 2017; 10:15 p.m.
Steve to Mom
Hope all is well with you I saw Tom and Crystal about a week ago

Mom to Steve
Thank you for letting me know; how does Crystal look?

Steve to Mom
She looked a lot better than I thought she would. she look good other than standing in the middle of the road panhandling. If you ever need anything just let me know. When was the last time you talk to

Mom to Steve
A couple of weeks ago by text; she had a phone she wanted me to activate and pay for; I tried to activate but she gave me wrong numbers! Told her where to look to

NO WIN

find the numbers and she said "thanks for helping"...
never heard back! The way it goes... thanks for letting
me know she seems ok!

January 30, 2017; 2:50 p.m.
Mom to Crystal   *(720.951.XXXX)*
This is Crystal's mom trying to call her back

January 31, 2017; 2:42 p.m.
Crystal to Mom   *(505.399.XXXX)*
What's up mama?
This is Crystal sorry this might be a different number I forgot.

Mom to Crystal
This is a different number. I didn't. Is this the one you need me to pay?

Crystal to Mom
Yes please mom... The # is 5052033783 Thanks Mom. I really miss all of you.

Mom to Crystal
I need to know the carrier and sign in information if you have been paying it on line. Whose name it the phone in?

Crystal to Mom
The service provider is cricket the name is Thomas key this is the number we haven't paid online... ever... so that should be all brand new. I have only paid with

SURRENDER

a prepaid cricket card from Walmart... so it's just a prepaid phone not attached to any account... please let us know if you have any questions... lots of love and hugs to you and the family... I miss Sage so much a can't hardly stand it. We won't have Wi-Fi for a bit so I will check the phone messages when we have it again.

February 1, 2017; 9:56 p.m.
Mom to Crystal   *(505.203.XXXX)*
I paid $50; hope it is working

Crystal to Mom
Yes it is on. Thank you very much mother. And Tom said thank you also.

February 25, 2017; 12:05 p.m.
Mom to Crystal   *(505.203.XXX)*
Just wanted to see if you still had this phone and if you are okay. Love you, mom

February 25, 2017; 7:03 p.m.
Crystal to Mom   *(505.203.XXXX)*
Yes we do, Mamma thank you very much. I'm OK just freezing and trying to figure out a program but still need my drivers license to do any program
Is there any chance you could put a credit card number on a hotel room that we are buying with reward points... we just need a card to keep on file... for accidentals. It's freezing cold outside and our current house situation has been put on hold for a few days.

NO WIN

Mom to Crystal
Yes, I will need the hotel information

Crystal to Mom
Sweet thank you so very much . . . I will have the information you need within the next few hours . . . the hotel is best western on pan American freeway

February 25, 2017; 8:47 p.m.
Crystal to Mom   (505.203.XXXX)
OK . . . if you could please get online and make a reservation under my friend . . . Sharon Martinez for best western on the pan American highway in Albuquerque nm and hold it with your card . . . then call me when you've booked it for tonight

Mom to Crystal
Online it says there are no rooms currently available; I will call. They will normally not allow me to give my credit card without authorization since you have to show the card. If you are paying with points, you will need to call and get the authorization form and send it back to them.
I called and they have no rooms for tonight. It appears they do have rooms for tomorrow night

Crystal to Mom
No worries . . . I will call you tomorrow

Mom to Crystal
Ok, love you

SURRENDER

February 28, 2017; 7:42 p.m.
Crystal to Mom   *(505.203.XXXX)*
A Cricket reminder. Your month of service is up tonight. Keep it going by paying BEFORE 11;59 p.m.
Hi mom . . . I am hoping for a bit of help paying the phone bill

Mom to Crystal
I will take care of it when I get home

March 1, 2017; 12:04 p.m.
Crystal to Mom   *(505.203.XXXX)*
Thanks mom

March 21, 2017; 7:29 p.m.
Mom to Crystal   *(505.203.XXXX)*
Crystal, Is this still your phone?

April 8, 2017; 4:30 p.m.
Mom to Crystal   *(505.203.XXXX)*
Trying to reach Crystal. Is this still her phone?

April 14, 2017; 6:42 p.m.
Mom to Steve
Any chance you've seen Crystal? Haven't heard from her in 7 or so weeks . . . usually hear around the first to pay her phone but no response from the numbers I have

Steve to Mom
I saw Tom riding a bicycle through town a few days ago

NO WIN

Mom to Steve
Hmmmm. I wonder if he is still with Crystal? The phone I was paying for was his!

Steve to Mom
Is the number still good give me the number I'll call it
I called and left a message
I'll keep my eye out for Tom next time I see him I'll flag him down

April 25, 2017; 12:37 p.m.
Mom to Steve
Just checking back to see if you heard anything about Crystal

Steve to Mom
No I've asked a couple people will check again today

April 27, 2017; 11:40 a.m.
Steve to Mom
Did not see them in Carlisle on freeway
I'll let you know if I find out anything

April 27, 2017; 2:52 p.m.
Mom to Steve
I didn't find a record of them at either hospital

April 29, 2017; 8:46 p.m.
Mom to Jim and Emma
Just got off the phone with Crystal. She sounds fine.

SURRENDER

Wants me to pay for a hotel tonight since it is snowing there. Waiting to see if she gets the paperwork to me. Same old same old!

April 30, 2017; 9:11 a.m.
Emma to Mom
Sounds about right. I'm glad she is okay at least Thank you for the update. I love you

(What I know now but didn't know then is that Crystal was already pregnant.)

Mom to Emma
Ended up calling the hotel and arranging it through some hokey system! I think it was the only reason she called but at least she is fine. I'm mad when she doesn't call and often madder when she does. No win with a heroin addict!

I had to make this reservation online and then write out an explanation of who would be checking in and my relationship to them. I ended up saying that Crystal Champ would be checking in with or without an ID and that she might be with a male named Tom Key, with or without an ID. When they checked in, the hotel manager called and asked for an additional deposit for miscellaneous expenses—or damage! I ended up with an extra twenty-five-dollar charge. I think they probably took the towels.

I spoke with Crystal on her birthday and she was super excited because a woman had given her sixty dollars while she was panhandling! Happy Birthday! I was grateful.

NO WIN

When Crystal was living on the streets and panhandling for her drugs and survival, I changed my attitude toward the folks on the corners in Dallas. Each time I gave money to someone waving a sign, I hoped someone was doing the same for Crystal. I know how irritating and uncomfortable it is to sit at a red light in a busy intersection and have a dirty, homeless person at your window with a sign pleading for money. Inside our air-conditioned cars with our music blaring, we sit staring ahead hoping the light will turn green. We don't want to look at their faces or question how they got there. We certainly don't want to entertain the thought that our lives could take the unimaginable turn that could leave us in their place. The reality is that we live in a broken world screaming for compassion.

Every organization that works with the homeless tells you not to give a homeless person money. I know, like Crystal, that they are most likely buying drugs or alcohol, but I just couldn't help myself. I saw her in their eyes, and it made me feel like I was doing something to help.

Not a single child lists "heroin addict" as what they want to be when they grow up. Crystal didn't want this life, and in my calmer moments, I knew that, but the longer she was on the streets, the harder it was to remember.

CHAPTER 17

HEROIN BABY

Sometime in June I found out that Crystal was pregnant. Steve in New Mexico was the one who told me. Normally we texted, but for this revelation, he called. He had seen Crystal panhandling on the highway and said she was visibly pregnant. He had tried to circle around to talk to her, but when he got back, she was gone. The news sent me reeling. I couldn't believe it!

I called and talked to Emma. I wasn't sure what to do. I was trying to get confirmation before I said anything to Jim or anyone else, but by the time I called him, Jim already knew. Crystal had called and told him directly. He was irritated that I had not informed him as soon as I heard the news, but it was a big bombshell to drop without being 100 percent sure. I was also trying to digest the information myself. In retrospect, I suppose I should have asked why he didn't call me as soon as he found out.

I was furious. The idea that Crystal was actively using heroin while pregnant made me sick to my stomach. I hated what she was doing to herself and the life she was living, but putting that pain on another person, especially a baby, seemed criminal. I kept thinking of all the women I knew who were struggling to get pregnant, and here was Crystal, pregnant and poisoning her child. I had carried six babies, and I was unnerved by the news.

I went to the internet and read countless articles about heroin babies. None of it sounded good. By all accounts, Crystal's newborn's first experience with life would be the horrible pain of withdrawal. Long-term effects were still unknown, but it sounded like this child could have a rough road ahead. I talked to all the kids, and we talked as we always talk. Two of my sons wouldn't even discuss it, they were so angry. My emotions were all over the place, and my daughters were also struggling to make sense of the news. There was nothing I could do. This was truly out of my hands. The fixer could not fix this.

Crystal finally texted and told me about the pregnancy and said she was planning on putting the baby up for adoption. I felt some relief that she was not planning to keep the baby. I didn't ask if she was still using; I knew she was. As upset as I was about the pregnancy, I was also scared for Crystal. She had gone through a tough delivery with Sage that ended in an emergency C-section. I did not want her to go into labor in the streets. She assured me she was working with a good adoption agency. All I could do was hope and pray.

On July 29, 2017, we all headed back to Ponte Vedra for another family week at the beach. Jim and Sage were joining us again, and Sage was excited to be with her cousins. It all felt so normal despite Crystal's absence and her pregnancy hanging in the back of our minds. The longer she was away, the more ethereal her presence became. The year before, I could still imagine her voice and picture her sitting at the table working a jigsaw puzzle. Now, she felt more like a shadow.

We had the usual group, plus my daughter Angie brought

her new boyfriend. We topped out at thirteen adults, five kids, and two dogs. I moved to the resort to stay in a hotel room. We had officially outgrown the rental house. I bought the girls matching blue-and-white-striped twirl dresses for our group picture, and they were adorable. I figured it was the last time I would convince my oldest granddaughter to wear a matching dress, but they were cute!

I needed the consistency of the beach that year—same beach, same rental, same people. Having Jim and Sage there for a third year in a row felt right, and it never occurred to me that things might change. Everyone was happy to be back together. Amanda was in Florida visiting her dad, but she drove over for the day so Ryan could see Sage and the other kids.

From the moment Ryan arrived, Sage had eyes for no one else. I think it was the first time Jim had really seen the connection between those two. They held hands and ran in the waves. They laid in the shallow water face-to-face and giggled as the waves washed over their bodies. That day belonged to Ryan, and then she went back to playing with her cousins.

The kids were all more comfortable with each other that summer, and also with their aunts and uncles. Luke loved body surfing with his Uncle Paul, and Aunt Angie couldn't get enough of Cameron and Sage. The little girls ran freely between each other's rooms, rummaging through their suitcases to try on princess dresses and trade out clothes and shoes. Sage was as relaxed and happy as I had ever seen her, and Jim appeared more comfortable as well. It was sad to leave and go back to reality. In reality Crystal was still pregnant, and her due date was closing in.

In early September Crystal reached out to me. She wanted to

SURRENDER

see if I could get her passport and birth certificate from Jim. She had given these documents to him for safekeeping, but now she needed them to get an ID. Crystal said she needed an ID to finalize her adoption—I'm not sure that was true, but it was what I believed at the time.

This had been an ongoing battle between Jim and me for the last couple of years. I had tried to reclaim Crystal's documents several times when she had asked for them, but Jim would not turn them over to me. Jim didn't want to give them to Crystal either. Before, I had just let it go, but now she apparently needed them to finalize an adoption.

Crystal was born in Canada and had always maintained her Canadian citizenship. Jim wanted to ensure that Sage could claim dual citizenship before giving the passport back to me or Crystal. He said Canadian citizenship was the only thing that Crystal might ever give her daughter, and he wasn't willing to give that up. He also figured she would only lose the documents.

I understood Jim's point, but Crystal was a grown woman, and if she wanted her passport, he needed to give it to her. I also did not want anything to get in the way of an adoption. After going back and forth, Jim agreed to go and apply for Sage's Canadian passport and then turn the documents over to me.

September 12, 2017; 1:56 p.m.
Mom to Crystal   *(505.544.XXXX)*
Jim is bringing your birth certificate and passport to me today and I will send them off to the address you provided to him. I will enclose a return envelope with postage.

After you get your ID, I would encourage you to mail them back to me so I can hold them for safekeeping in the event you need them again. I hope you are well. Love you

September 14, 2017; 12:44 p.m.
Mom to Crystal   ***(505.544.XXXX)***
Your papers should be at the adoption agency tomorrow, birth certificate and passport. I do not have your social security card but Mick was able to use a W2 that had his ss# so I sent an old W2 and an old tax return

Crystal to Mom
Thank you so much mom

    It was at this point that I started communicating with the adoption agency directly. Once I had the name of the agency, I went online and did some research. I wanted to be sure that Crystal was using a legitimate agency that would take care of both Crystal and the baby. It was a faith-based adoption agency, and it looked like they were doing good work. I spoke with Carmen, who was the person working with Crystal and Tom. She was very reassuring.
    She said many of their adoptions involved opioid-addicted mothers, and they had multiple families willing to welcome those babies into their homes. She said Crystal and Tom were looking at family albums of prospective parents but hadn't been able to decide on a family. She said they had spent hours pouring over the possible families, and she had finally let them take three books with them in the hopes they would be able to

decide. She was putting them up at a hotel at the time we were corresponding.

September 22, 2017; 10:26 a.m.
Mom to Crystal (505.544.XXXX)
Carmen from the adoption agency called and is trying to get in touch with you. She has your documents. Please stay in touch and let me know when the baby is born so I know you are safe. Love you

Crystal to Mom
Ok xo
Crystal

On September 23, Officer Ryan Holets found Crystal in an alley in Albuquerque shooting up heroin and offered to adopt her baby. She accepted his offer. I would not know this until the story broke on CNN on December 1, 2017. I didn't hear from Crystal again until October 24, despite reaching out to her multiple times.

I reached out to the adoption agency on several occasions to try and find out what was going on. Carmen told me that Tom had met with her and returned the family books, but Crystal was not with him. He did not communicate one way or the other if they had decided on a family. I kept reaching out, and Crystal kept ignoring me.

There's nothing more irritating than a mother who just keeps asking questions no matter how much you try to ignore her, and then when you give her the short answer, she just continues to ask more questions. That was me. I needed to know that Crystal and the baby were safe.

HEROIN BABY

September 28, 2017; 9:37 p.m.
Mom to Crystal   (505.544.XXXX)
Adoption agency said you have not picked up your documents to get an ID. Are you still planning to move forward with the adoption?

October 2, 2017; 11:29 a.m.
Mom to Crystal   (505.544.XXXX)
Is this still your phone? Have you gotten documents from Carmen? Please get things in order so you can deliver in a safe place.

October 24, 2017; 12:25 p.m.
Mom to Crystal   (505.544.XXXX)
How are you? Is this still Crystal's phone? Are you in touch with Adoption agency? Please deliver in a safe place for you and the baby.

October 24, 2017; 3:49 p.m.
Crystal to Mom   (505.544.XXXX)
Yes this is my phone still mom . . . I had a beautiful baby girl on October 12 and my labour only lasted for 6-7 hours before having a natural birth . . . the adoption went well and her parents named her Hope Crystal . . . im very busy but will email you pics later when im around wifi if you remind me of your email addresses

Mom to Crystal
I am glad you had a safe and easier delivery and that all went well with the adoption. Any luck getting clean? I love you

SURRENDER

Crystal never sent me pictures or gave me any additional information on the baby. I called Carmen at the adoption agency to thank her and see if I could get any more information. Carmen said they had not done the adoption through her. I didn't know what to think or where the baby was, but my mind went to some pretty dark places. I have no idea if she ever picked up her documents.

October 25, 2017; 6:42 p.m.
Mom to Crystal   (505.544.XXXX)
Talked to Carmen at the adoption agency and she said you checked out of the hotel and she was unaware that you had delivered. Who did you do the adoption through? Were you able to get an ID?

Crystal to Mom
We had explored different possible options for the adoption . . . why would you contact Carmen?

Mom to Crystal
That's the contact you gave me, that is where I sent your documents. I texted her to thank her for her help

October 25, 2017; 9:05 p.m.
Crystal to Mom   (505.544.XXXX)
Mom that sounds like a bunch of BS . . . Im Sincerely shocked that you felt it necessary to get information from the coordinator of one of the possible options . . . we checked out of the hotel because it was time to check out and Carmen was unaware of the whole situation because she was not our choice.

There is absolutely no reason for you to contact Carmen
... if you needed to get an update or understanding
of the situation with my life wouldn't it be 4 the best
that you ask me questions about the adoption and
not a stranger? As for my ID ... I will have to get the
money and the rest of my proof together and get my
resident alien card and Canadian passport renewed and
my driver's license isn't expired ... I just need proof of
residence ... I still have my important documents and it's
just going to take a bit to get the money together ...

Mom to Crystal
Chill out! I have texted you numerous times with no
response. Even knowing my concerns for you, you had the
baby two weeks ago and didn't even bother to tell me. I
had looked up her agency and was impressed with the
work they were doing and happy that you had found this
place ... not knowing anything different, I simply reached
out to thank her. I hope you found the baby a good home.
   Maybe try stepping back sometime and thinking
about what the people who love you have gone through
over the last few years. I wouldn't have to reach out to
strangers if you would stay in touch.

Crystal to Mom
I can't get these downloads because I don't have data or
wifi just

Mom to Crystal
It's a text message

SURRENDER

November 12, 2017; 10:20 p.m.
Mom to Crystal   *(505.544.XXXX)*
Did you ever figure out how to read my text messages? I would appreciate if you would give me updates of where you are and if you are okay. Love you

Crystal to Mom
Surviving

November 13, 2017; 1:55 p.m.
Mom to Crystal   *(505.544.XXXX)*
Okay, please try and stay in touch. Love you

CHAPTER 18

FROM CNN TO MENDING FENCES

December 1, 2017; 6:57 a.m.
Jordan to Mom
Hi. Can you call me as soon as you're awake? It's not an emergency. Everyone is fine, but I need to talk to you.

I called Jordan back. He was at the gym working out. He had just seen Crystal on CNN—images of her shooting up in an alley and being confronted by a policeman. He sent me and Emma the screen shots on the next page that he took during the broadcasts while he was working out. The captions tell it all!

December 1, 2017; 7:22 a.m.
Emma to Mom and Jordan
Wow. So insane. Thanks for capturing this. Love you

Mom to Jordan and Emma
Breaks my heart but relieved to know the baby is safe!
Thanks for screen shots!
Love you both

SURRENDER

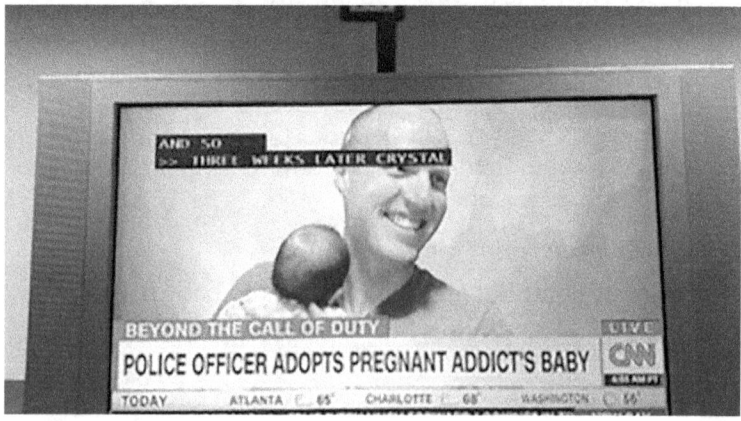

FROM CNN TO MENDING FENCES

December 1, 2017; 7:16 a.m.
Mom to Crystal   (505.544.XXXX)
Jordan just called and said he saw you on CNN this morning and a policeman adopted your baby ... big human interest story. Why didn't you just tell me? Hope you are okay.

Crystal to Mom
Yep ... it was serendipity the family named her Hope Crystal and had no idea my real name is Hope ... Ryan and Rebecca are wonderful people and they are going to wonderful parents that care about Hope but also Tom and me.

Mom to Crystal
Glad she found a good home, and you have always had lots of people who care about you ... you just need to decide to care about yourself.
Mom

SURRENDER

Crystal to Mom
Yes the irony of my tragedy

December 1, 2017; 9:21 a.m.
Mom to Jordan and Emma
This story has been picked up by all the news feeds so I will need to call the family and give them a heads up before they just see it . . . Crystal is now the poster child for sad addicted pregnant mothers!

December 12, 2017; 4:50 p.m.
Mom to Crystal (505.544.XXXX)
Just heard you are on your way to Florida to rehab. Hope it's true Please confirm. Mom

6:25 p.m.
Crystal to Mom
How did you hear that?

7:42 p.m.
Mom to Crystal
Media . . . Your all over Facebook etc. is it true or just BS? I do consider you mine even if you have moved on so would like to know the truth rather than being contacted by old friends and media outlets. I don't talk to anyone. Don't want to be a story. My focus is on protecting Sage.

December 12, 2017; 10:02 p.m.
Mom to Crystal (505.544.XXXX)
Are you going to rehab or not? Give me that much

FROM CNN TO MENDING FENCES

December 13, 2017; 2:09 a.m.
Crystal to Mom   (505.544.XXXX)
Yes . . . We are researching our options for full rides . . . which are a few . . . As for the follow up interview with CNN . . . You where mentioned because of some of the questions asked by the reporter . . . not sure what will be there in the final product on CNN but I had agreed to be interviewed again. Sorry if it causes you any issues . . . that was never my intention. Love you . . . hopefully we will be heading to rehab by the end of the week

11:13 a.m.
Mom to Crystal
Please let me know when and where you go. I hope in some bizarre way this becomes an incentive for you to get clean

10:36 p.m.
Mom to Crystal
The guy who interviewed you emailed me today and wanted to talk. Of course, he's from Lakewood . . . what are the chances. I told him no, but he then volunteered to keep me in the loop on you! I would prefer for you to give me the information. He said lots of people had been offering rehab and I didn't want to tell him that we had been offering rehab for the last 3 years and you had no interest! I hope that with the media focus that maybe you will be able to make choices to change your life. You could have a real future! I hope the best for you, but I also hope you will protect Sage by leaving her out of your conversations

SURRENDER

... I've cried a lot today ... for you, for Sage ... the other daughter you seem to forget. I ask as you become an internet star that you protect her. I hope your other daughter is in a safe and positive environment and I only wish you recovery and life. I love you. Wish I didn't ... this would all hurt so much less if I didn't love you so much. Take care

December 15, 2017; 10:08 p.m.
Mom to Crystal   (505.544.XXXX)
I saw the follow up story today. I hope you will seriously consider rehab. Right now there are multiple options because of this focus on you and it is a real opportunity. We both know what rehab is about ... painful, hard, a true change in the way you are living your life, but you could have a wonderful life on the other side of heroin ... it doesn't love you like your family. The choice is yours beautiful girl ... not CNN or anyone else. You are sick; you have an addiction. No matter what you decide, I will always love you. Mom

On December 25, 2017, Crystal called me from Mending Fences, a drug rehabilitation facility in Morriston, Florida, near Ocala. I already knew she was there and had done some research on the facility. They used horses as part of the rehabilitation, and I knew Crystal would like that. Mending Fences had given both Crystal and Tom full rides for rehab. My understanding was the costs was around $100,000 each. Pretty amazing!

On Christmas morning I was sitting on my bed chatting with Emma and Angie and enjoying our time together before the rest of the family descended. The phone rang. I saw the area code and knew immediately it was Crystal. She sounded good—almost childlike. She told me she was through the initial detox and felt OK. I put her on speakerphone so we could all talk, and she went on to describe the facility. She said it was beautiful; she loved the horses and the openness, and she liked Florida. Her counselor was also named Crystal, and she felt that they had a good connection and this Crystal would really help her. Even in that first conversation, she told me she was planning on staying in Ocala, where they had a large sober-living community. I was grateful that she was not planning on going back to New Mexico.

She said the food was great, and she was especially excited about the oatmeal bar with all its various toppings. She was giggling as she told me how much I would like it. She said they didn't have to do chores and it wasn't anything like her other rehab experience. At Mending Fences, her only job was to focus on herself and getting clean. That's what $100,000 rehab can get you! She had a horse to take care of, yoga classes, swimming, hiking, healthy food, and therapy. I was impressed. It certainly wasn't the kind of rehab that I was ever going to be able to give her. Thank you, CNN. Crystal said she put me on the list to receive information and be able to check on her. Unlike at Hoy, she had very flexible phone time, but could only talk for fifteen minutes. She wished us a Merry Christmas and hung up.

It took me less than ten minutes to forget my anger and fall back in love with Crystal—just like I had when she was sixteen. Hearing from Crystal was a wonderful Christmas gift, and I was grateful.

I called Mending Fences a few days later to check on how she was doing. They gave me no information and wouldn't acknowledge that she was even there. They took my name and number, and Crystal called me back later that day. This was a completely different Crystal than the one I had talked to on Christmas. She

SURRENDER

sounded irritated, and it was clear that Tom was standing next to her during the conversation. The little girl happy voice was gone and her "street voice" and demeanor were back.

I told her I had called to check on how she was doing and that she truly did not need to call me back if she didn't want to. I certainly wasn't looking to put any pressure on her. I was just grateful she was off the streets and safe. We talked for a few more minutes before she said she had to go to yoga and hung up. That was my last phone call from Mending Fences.

I had very little additional communication with Crystal during rehab. There were a few emails, and I knew she was also in touch with her sister Emma. I didn't call back. I felt like it was Crystal's choice when and if she wanted to connect with me. I thought I needed to give her distance to do the arduous work of getting clean. Crystal had been on the streets for over two years at that point. The adjustment to being safe, having access to clean clothes, a bed, and food must have been overwhelming, but addressing the demons that kept her using was the big hurdle, and I didn't want to get in the way.

I also had my own adjusting to do. I had been living in a constant state of worry and trauma since August 2015 when she started using again. Rationally I knew that Crystal being safely tucked away in rehab was a good thing. Getting clean had always been the goal. So many prayers from so many people that Crystal would find a way to get clean. I believe in the power of prayer and I believe in miracles. I had prayed and prayed, but in my wildest dreams I could not have predicted the series of events that eventually landed her at Mending Fences. I had hoped for a miracle, and when it happened, I was truly not prepared for what would come next.

CHAPTER 19

ANGER

Once Crystal was safe, I began to experience a rage inside myself that I never knew I was capable of. I had been on an emotional roller coaster for five years, and I now had a strong urge to punch something or someone. It was a very bizarre feeling. I felt as though my heart was going to jump out of my chest and the knot in my stomach would not relax. I amped up my workouts. Anger, fear, love, irritation, grief, disappointment—so many emotions I had been stuffing down inside myself. Now those emotions were fighting to explode to the surface. I found the most shocking words coming out of my mouth! I became sarcastic, cynical, and judgmental. It wasn't me. I turned to prayer and meditation in search of compassion and forgiveness. Crystal was an addict who had a disease. I believed that, and I needed to remember it.

I think my anger was a symptom of how out of control I felt. With Crystal in rehab, everything had turned upside down, and I was having trouble regaining my footing. Crystal living on the streets had become my "norm," and I was accustomed to that normality. The way I was living my life was not great, but I felt

SURRENDER

some sense of control in that living. Basically I had shut down my emotions, limited the people I allowed into my circle, spent time with Sage, worked, and worked out.

My clients had become my social outlet, but most clients aren't long-term relationships. You date them seriously, but you don't marry them. It was the perfect kind of relationship for me: business-based with not too much depth. Not an ideal existence, but one I could manage. I talked to God a lot, much more than I talked to anyone else. I trusted God to keep my secrets. He did an excellent job... until he didn't. I guess God was pretty fed up with the way I was living my life as well.

In early January 2018, the CNN story was replayed again as part of *Megan Kelly TODAY*. I was lying on the floor stretching out before getting ready for work—my usual morning routine. I glanced up at the TV from my position on the floor and saw Megan Kelley interviewing Ryan Holets, the policeman who had adopted Crystal's baby. Once again I watched the video of pregnant Crystal shooting up in an alley next to Tom, crying with the cameras in her face. Megan interviewed Ryan, and then his wife, Rebecca—holding Crystal's baby—joined in the conversation. Hope was almost four months old now and just beautiful. They all looked happy. At the end of the interview, Megan Kelly showed a picture of Crystal and Tom at Mending Fences, standing in a lovely field with their horses. Crystal was smiling and looked healthy. I wanted to throw something at the TV. It seemed that each time I would start to regain my footing, the story would show up again, and each time I would dissolve into tears.

On January 30, 2018, Ryan, Rebecca, and Hope were invited to the State of the Union Address as Melania Trump's guest. I was given a heads-up by friends and chose to attend my Bible

ANGER

study and skip the address. I was beginning to wonder if this would be my new norm—watching Hope grow up on national television. For whatever reason, it just didn't sit right with me. All I could think about was Sage and how hard we had worked to keep her out of the spotlight.

For the next few months, I bounced between extreme anger and extreme fear. As scared as I had been for the last two-and-a-half years that Crystal would never get clean and die on the streets, I was now equally as scared of what it would mean if she did get clean. Would she want to be part of my life? Was there enough forgiveness in the world for that to happen? Would she want to be part of Sage's life? Would Jim allow it? All these things were scary to consider. I had not seen Crystal since August 2015. Our communication had consisted predominately of texts centered around Crystal getting what she needed from me. I had no idea who this Crystal was.

While Crystal was doing work at Mending Fences, I was trying to do some work on myself. I found I was still having a tough time reaching out to people, so I started listening to books. I ordered audiobooks and listened to podcasts by various spiritual leaders. Now my workouts included inspirational listening. I found plenty of information on the power of forgiveness and compassion, along with lots of good "come back" stories. I listened to Thich Nhat Hanh speak on compassionate listening and I started trying to implement some of his practices such as mindful breathing and deep listening. I turned off the television and started writing this book. What I was unable to share with people, I wrote about in this book.

I worked at slowing down, not in the sense of work, but in the sense of movement. I have always moved too fast and

SURRENDER

without focus, which explains the constant bruises on my body with no memory of how I got them. I tried doing the same thing with driving, but I'm not sure I'm succeeding there. I'm not a great driver and have always been a curb hitter. I blame part of it on driving too fast and lack of focus, but there's also the short thing—I simply cannot see the front of my car.

I have started turning my phone off or muting it at night. That probably sounds ridiculous, but it was a huge thing for me. With so many children out in the world for so many years, I had always left my phone on in case of an emergency. While Crystal was on the streets, I had never wanted to be unavailable, so I continued the habit. Now Crystal was in sober living and safe. My oldest child was forty-one and my youngest was twenty-eight. If someone had a problem between 10:00 p.m. and 7:00 a.m., they could call each other. Setting boundaries . . . so new!

It was also time to take a hard look at my other behaviors. I had spent years talking about relinquishing control and reciting the serenity prayer, but in truth I was still hanging on and trying to control the outcomes in my life. I wanted Crystal clean; I had been praying for years that she would kick her addiction—but this was not the scenario I had written. I wanted God to save her, but I wanted him to save her on my terms, and my terms did not involve a policeman and CNN!

I also needed to admit that I had some big ego issues of my own to deal with. For many years, I had been the fixer in Crystal's life . . . her angel. It made me feel special, but in a dysfunctional way. I had taken her into my home at sixteen when her adoptive parents had thrown her away. I had nurtured her as part of my family and loved her as my child. I had driven to Santa Fe in

ANGER

2013, pulled her off the floor, and gotten her into detox and rehab. I had been there through her first pregnancy and delivery, and I had continued to be there when she walked out on her family and chose the streets and heroin over her precious child.

Now she was on national television proclaiming that Ryan was her angel! Just like that, I was knocked off my cloud and stripped of my wings. I had bought phones, paid bills, booked hotels, and always responded when she reached out. I never closed the door and always told her I loved her, but what I couldn't do was get her into rehab.

Getting Crystal into rehab took a policeman, a needle, a baby, CNN, and a viral news story. At first, in my anger, I would simply say, "My daughter made a good business decision." Pregnant in an alley with a needle in her arm and confronted by a policeman, what would you choose—jail or adoption? Adoption by a policeman seemed like the best choice to me. Crystal had already done jail twice, and I'm sure the idea of doing it pregnant was terrifying. As my anger cooled, I worked toward developing gratitude and an attitude adjustment. There's no telling where the baby would have ended up if she had gone to jail.

Crystal's addiction and subsequent path was not about me. It never had been. I was not responsible for putting the needle in her arm, and I was not responsible for taking it out. Everything I did while Crystal was on her journey—from buying phones to paying for hotels to constantly responding to text messages—was about me and my need to fix and save. It was also about maintaining the image that I *could* fix and save. Who was I if I couldn't save my own daughter? That was a scary realization. I had tied my own self-worth to my ability to save an addict. That was crazy thinking. Back to the Serenity Prayer.

SURRENDER

I think it was the helplessness and complete lack of control that caused the anger and grief to rage inside of me; the CNN story merely triggered it. I was grateful to CNN and their efforts. They had given Crystal an amazing opportunity to get clean. All I could do now was hope she wouldn't blow it. Despite the massive media coverage, which I still hated, I did believe that Ryan and Rebecca acted out of compassion when they offered to adopt Crystal's baby, and I thought Hope was very lucky to be in their home.

For the last five years, my life had revolved around Crystal's addiction and the fallout from her choices. I had sworn that I would not let Crystal's addiction destroy me or my family, but none of it was ever within my control. I thought that by including Jim and Sage in our family, I could help to ease their loss and pain as well, but I couldn't. We all got hurt. I had focused so much on Crystal's addiction that I missed my own obsession with the situation. It was no one's intention to hurt me. Not Crystal, not CNN, not Ryan or any of the other contributors to "the saving of Crystal." I was just collateral damage along with Jim, Sage, and my family.

God had given me what I wanted, but he had given it to me in a way that I could claim absolutely no ownership. What a clever God! Ultimately I contributed nothing to "the saving of Crystal," and yet she was saved. (At least that's how it felt at the time.) It was time to forgive myself for my inability to save Crystal and accept that she had never been mine to save in the first place. Crystal was only on loan to me! Like all children, she belonged only to herself.

I reread Kahlil Gibran's poem, "On Children":

ANGER

And a woman who held a babe against her bosom said,
"Speak to us of children." And he said:
Your children are not your children.
They are the sons and daughters of Life's longing for itself.
They come through you but not from you,
And though they are with you, yet they belong not to you.

You may give them your love but not your thoughts.
For they have their own thoughts.
You may house their bodies but not their souls,
For their souls dwell in the house of tomorrow,
Which you cannot visit, not even in your dreams.
You may strive to be like them, but seek not to make them like you.
For life goes not backward nor tarries with yesterday.

You are the bows from which your children as living arrows are sent forth.
The archer sees the mark upon the path of the infinite,
And he bends you with His might that His arrows may go swift and far.
Let your bending in the archer's hand be for gladness;
For even as He loves the arrow that flies,
So He loves also the bow that is stable.

—*The Prophet*, published 1923

CHAPTER 20

BROKEN

Crystal called me on April 7, 2018, to tell me she had been released from Mending Fences and was now living in a sober housing facility in Ocala with some other girls. We ended up talking for almost an hour, and it felt good to catch up. She and Tom had parted ways. They had gone through a final therapy session together before he left Mending Fences to say goodbye and establish boundaries for their relationship. They had agreed not to see each other for a year. I thought that was good news. Mending Fences had accomplished with Crystal and Tom what I had been unable to do with Crystal and Jim.

We talked about the family, and then we talked a lot about Sage. That was easy; I could talk about Sage all day. Crystal wanted to hear stories, and I had plenty! Crystal thanked me for spending time with Sage and asked me to thank Mick and Amanda as well. She said she had been in touch with Jim a couple of times—it didn't sound like it had gone great. Crystal reiterated how fortunate she was to be in a place where she was receiving good and consistent counseling. She said there was always someone to call her out on her bullshit. She knew Jim

SURRENDER

had not been given the same opportunity, and she recognized it was going to be a tough road ahead for the two of them. I was having my own tough road with Jim, but I didn't feel it was the right time to go into that with Crystal. I told her I loved her and was proud of her, and we said good-bye.

After Crystal and Tom entered Mending Fences, my relationship with Jim took a turn. I will never know exactly where all the paranoia came from, and honestly I think he was just scared—scared of losing Sage, of what Crystal's sobriety would mean for him, and of confronting his own demons. I could relate. Over the years there had been moments when Jim came at me with suspicions about this or that, but we had always been able to talk our way through it. This time was different. Crystal was in rehab, and Jim reacted by pulling Sage close and battening down the hatches of his life. With no explanation that made sense to me, I suddenly found myself on the outside looking in.

In retrospect, we should have all marched ourselves into therapy as soon as Crystal started using again, but we didn't. We should have prepared ourselves to deal with the various contingencies that would inevitably come up. A year or so into her time on the streets, a part of me had just given up. I think I was more prepared for the scenario in which Crystal died than the one where she would get clean and show up in my life again. I don't believe Jim was any more equipped than I was.

When Jim first arrived in Dallas, I had encouraged him to try an Al-Anon or a Narcotics Anonymous meeting. I felt like he really needed to talk to someone about what he was going through. He had not even begun to reconcile all the craziness that had happened in his life. All his friends were back in Santa Fe. He tried attending a meeting, but it turned out to be sort of a disaster, and he didn't go back. He took Sage to therapy but not himself. There was a lot of unresolved anger there.

When Jim came for Christmas, while Crystal was at Mending Fences, he was different. I had hoped that when Sage was napping he would go have lunch with Emma and Mick and just talk, but he didn't want to put Sage down for a nap. He didn't want to let her out of his sight. The three of them took Sage to a restaurant down the street where she could play with other kids while they ate and talked. His paranoia was in overdrive, and he alluded to Emma and Mick that he felt I was trying to take Sage, to exert control over her life. My children knew that was ridiculous, but I had made a couple of decisions, which I thought would protect Sage, and Jim read them as just the opposite. The two of us reacted very differently to Crystal going into rehab, and my timing was bad.

Shortly after Crystal went into rehab, I set up a bank account in Sage's name so family members could contribute to it rather than buying her toys she didn't need. Sue and I had set it up together. My kids were always trying to come up with ways to help Jim, and the bank account seemed like an easy answer. It wasn't new information. I had been talking to him about it for months, but Sue and I needed to go to the bank together, so it had taken until the week before Christmas for our schedules to work. Jim was not happy and got upset with me for using Sage's social security number without his permission. He said he didn't want her identity "out there." I reminded him that she was in school and had medical insurance. Both the school and the insurance company had her social security number. Still, it didn't sit well with him.

When they came back from lunch, we let Sage open some of

her Christmas presents since we would not see her on Christmas day. She was happy and playing, but every time she got settled into an activity or movie, Jim would get down on the floor and stir her up. It all felt very weird. At one point, Jim asked me how long I expected him to stay. I told him I had no expectations and he was free to leave whenever he wanted. I ended up not giving Sage my Christmas gift—it was just too awkward. I put her gift in the top of her closet, then rewrapped it and mailed it for her birthday in May.

Still, I tried to remain understanding. After all, we were both still reeling from the CNN story and subsequent Facebook postings and calls. Jim was trying to protect Sage and keep her away from the "story." I think the notion of sharing Sage with Crystal had him completely rattled. We were just not on the same page. Crystal had only been in rehab a couple of weeks, and I wasn't sure she would even stay. My level of cynicism was rather high at that point. I thought Crystal and Tom were just as likely to take the flight to Florida and bail as they were to stick with rehab. Winter in Florida was much more appealing than winter in New Mexico. I felt that we were a long way from allowing Crystal back into Sage's life. I naïvely thought there was a "we" where Sage was concerned.

Jim had periodically told me that if Crystal ever got clean and came back into my life, it would create a conflict between us. I didn't really understand what conflict he was so worried about. I was more connected to Jim at that point than I was to Crystal, and my primary concern had always been Sage and her best interest. Jim was a good dad, and I knew he was committed to Sage and providing her the best life possible. I had supported him in every way I could since his move to Dallas. That included his getting sole custody.

Crystal was the one who would need to earn back my trust. If there was going to be a conflict over Sage, I believed it would be between me and Crystal, not me and Jim. We had never had any major conflicts where Sage was concerned. I preferred the clothes and shoes I bought her to the ones he bought her, but that was merely a style choice. I thought she should sleep in her own bed, and she did at my house, but beyond that we were usually on the same page. We agreed on what mattered—that Sage was a most beautiful and spectacular child!

I wasn't unaware. I knew there were things that would have to change between us once Crystal was in rehab. For the past two and a half years, Jim and I had confided in each other on all things concerning Crystal. Now that Crystal was in rehab, that would need to change. My hope was that she would reach out to both of us, but I knew it would be in very different capacities. There would be times Crystal would call me and times she would call Jim. Now that she was in therapy, those conversations would need to be private as part of her recovery.

I restated again to Jim that decisions regarding Sage would need to be worked out between the two of them as her parents, but I would always be there for Sage. I hoped my words would reassure him as far as where I saw my relationship with Sage, but his response was not what I expected. He reminded me that, according to his custody order, I could not even send a picture of Sage to Crystal without his permission. That should have been a clue of where things were headed, but I was oblivious to what was coming.

Sage was an integral part of my life at that point. She had spent almost every weekend with me for the first year she was in Dallas. In 2017 we moved to an every-other-weekend schedule.

SURRENDER

Jim was working full-time during the week and wanted some full weekends with Sage. I understood, and we both tried to be flexible. There were times I might go three weeks without a visit, but never more than that.

Jim and Sage had spent the previous three summers coming to the beach for family vacations, and the kids had hung out together over the last two Thanksgivings. Sage had real relationships with her cousins, and they all considered each other as family. I was even hoping to take her to Denver with me on one of my upcoming visits so she could hang out with her cousins there. Sage had also developed a very tight relationship with sweet Ryan and Amanda and my son, Mick. They had spent time with Sage virtually every weekend she was with me. We were all heavily invested in Sage's life.

Starting in January 2018, Jim started canceling weekends. He would tell me they were sick, or he had made plans and forgotten to tell me. By mid-April, I had not seen Sage in five weeks and Mick moved to Denver without having a chance to say good-bye to the little girl he had spent so much time with. It was heartbreaking. Jim told me that he needed space with Sage while he adjusted to reconnecting with Crystal. He said he was preparing Sage for a separation from me and his mother and working toward a more permanent move away from Texas. My text messages became more pleading, and his became more condescending. He had all the power in this situation. It was a "no win" for me.

At the end of April, Jim and I finally spoke on the phone. Jim said that he wasn't saying I would never see Sage again, but he needed to do things according to his own timetable, and for the moment he needed to spend time with his daughter and prepare her for their move. He reminded me that I only saw my other grandchildren every few months, but it wasn't the same and he knew it. He went on to justify his decision by telling me that he had spoken with lots of people, and they all agreed he was doing the right thing. I asked where they were moving, and he said he was taking Sage to live in the Caribbean. I asked him why the Caribbean, and he said he had always wanted to raise Sage near the ocean. I cried, but there was nothing left to say.

After we hung up, I sat in the yard for a long time, pulling weeds and crying. I had no legal rights to Sage; I had always known that. I took the risk when I allowed myself to fall in love with her just as I had taken the risk when I fell in love with Crystal. Who could resist falling in love with such a precious child? She had lost her mother, and I wanted to be there in any way I could to fill that void. What I couldn't give to Crystal, I had hoped to give to Sage. Letting go is hard.

It was déjà vu! Just as I wished that I had known I would not see Crystal again after that day in August 2015, I wished that I had known that March 17 would be my last visit with Sage. It was a good weekend, but weekends with Sage were always special. We had done our usual routine, and after her nap she stood on my deck, holding a plastic rake as a guitar, and sang at the top of her lungs, "I am a rock star; I am a rock star!"

Having Sage ripped from my life with no warning has broken me, but I know I will heal. Months later, I still cry almost every day, and I wonder what she thinks. Her room and her butterfly bed are just as she left them, with stuffed animals and toys waiting. I have a tough time going in. It just hurts too much. My home is full of Sage memories . . . wonderful memories . . . laughing, dancing, watching movies, snuggling, and joy! I write

SURRENDER

cards every week, but I'm sure she's confused as to where I am. I hope she knows I didn't want to go away and that I love her. I don't want her left with the same abandonment issues as her mother.

Amanda still brings Ryan over to play, and Ryan constantly asks us where Sage is. He misses her too and doesn't understand where she went. It's hard to explain to a four-year-old where his best friend has gone. Her swim teacher for two years, her Sunday School teacher, my neighbors—they all ask. Nobody got to say good-bye.

I pray that Jim will find a way to cope with his fears and his paranoia, and not project them onto Sage. I worry he will smother her if he doesn't. It should not be a daughter's responsibility to save her father or carry his feelings, and children can sense those unhealed and unsaid emotions. I hope that Jim finds his way to peace and healing, so he can bring joy and light into Sage's life and help her to explore all the wonderful things this world has to offer. I can only hope that I have imprinted on her enough that she won't forget our time together. Jim says I will always be Sage's grandmother and he wants me to be in her life, but for now, he needs time and space. I can do nothing but respect his request and wait.

Like Crystal, Sage was never mine. She was a gift I held for a moment and then she was gone. A gift I could love and cherish, but she did not belong to me.

I am trying to release the anger I feel at losing Sage and look at Jim through a compassionate lens. Most days I still fail, but I know that he loves Sage and will do his best for her. I am trying to stay in a place of gratitude. I am thankful for the time I had with Sage and grateful that she has a father who loved her enough to put her first, even as his world was crumbling. I do have empathy for Jim and his situation. Having a heroin addict in your life, clean or using, is never easy or predictable. Whether in or out of Sage's life, no matter how long Crystal stays clean, Jim will always worry and live in fear of another relapse and how it will impact Sage and their lives.

When Crystal was on the streets, Jim would often downplay my role in Crystal's life and focus solely on his own pain and loss. He was the one who she had "done wrong." He was the one who would have to explain things to Sage, raise a child on his own, and protect her from the ramifications of Crystal's addiction. I listened and sympathized, but it hurt my feelings. I love Crystal too, and losing her to heroin and the streets has been painful for me as well. Jim and I are both casualties of Crystal's addiction, but I've come to accept that Jim's pain is different than mine. If Crystal chooses never to walk into my life again, it will hurt, but I will survive. I am a survivor, and I am at peace that I did everything possible to save her.

The long-term effects on Jim's life are more complicated, and I do not envy the road ahead for him. So long as Crystal is alive, clean or using, she will be Sage's mother, and Jim will need to deal with Crystal and the decision they made *together* to bring Sage into this world.

CHAPTER 21

GRIEVING AND HEALING

In life we grieve. We grieve death, divorce, friends, and losses of every kind both large and small. I have always found it harder to grieve the living than the dead—and I have grieved some dead! Death is generally out of our hands. We don't get to pick the time, date, or circumstances that remove a loved one from our lives. Death often comes as a surprise, and we are caught completely off guard by the loss. Other times we are relieved when the last breath is taken and suffering stops. Regardless, we grieve, and that process takes time.

The stages of grief—denial, anger, bargaining, depression, and acceptance—largely hold true as a path to healing. But even after decades of grieving and acceptance, I can find myself revisiting anger as I try to make sense of a loss—my sister's suicide, for example. I think suicide is one form of death that you just keep revisiting, trying to figure out a "why." Time does heal, but even after decades of working through grief, most of us are left with an empty hole where our loved one once lived.

I have certainly grieved Crystal over the last few years. I have tried to be aware of the stages and walk that linear path, one step at a time, to find healing. But unlike those I've lost to death, I just can't seem to get to the end where I find peace and acceptance. Crystal continues to be a walking and breathing cyclone in my life, and each time I think I have a step conquered, I get blown back to the beginning. It's like playing Candyland: every time I think I'm going to make it to the Candy Castle, I get thrown back into Molasses Swamp. This is the dilemma when you mourn the living.

I realize now that I hung out in "denial" a lot longer than I should have, and I'm not sure I will ever be able to give up the anger. Heroin took so much. I grieve the loss of what could have been, all the lost dreams and expectations of how you thought life would work out. Those are hard losses to get over. As I write this, I don't know who Crystal is today. I haven't seen her since 2015 and our communication generally has been brief and shallow. There is little communication between the two of us that I have not shared in this book. The Crystal I'm grieving is long gone, so I'm trying to be open to the Crystal who "is." It's a little tricky.

I am also grieving the loss of Sage and Jim in my life. Sage filled a void that helped me cope with losing her mother, and Jim was the only other person who could really share the craziness of stalking Crystal's addiction. I miss them both. When I felt helpless in my relationship with Crystal, nurturing Sage kept me sane and gave me purpose. Decorating her room, buying clothes and shoes, playing on the weekends, and simply being together, cuddling and talking, helped bring some light into my life when I had shut everyone else out. I can now accept that it was another form of denial, but I do miss her.

I do believe I will see Sage again, but we will have a very

different relationship than the one we've had since 2015. When I can move past my current sadness and tears, I am hopeful that I can accept that this change was necessary and would have happened whether Crystal got clean or not. I always knew Jim did not want to build a life in Dallas, and to his credit, I knew he would never be the type of person who would leave his daughter to pursue his own selfish path. It was inevitable that our relationship would change. I just wish we could have managed the transition in a better way.

I love being a grandmother, but I never wanted to raise my grandchildren. I don't need a "parenting do-over." I loved being a mother more than anything else I have ever done, but parenting my own menagerie of children was enough. Working two jobs and keeping Sage on the weekends was just another way for me to isolate from the world, and I don't think it was physically sustainable for me in the long term.

I will need time to grieve what I had with Sage. Cribs, diapers, big beds, and potty training—my role in Sage's life since 2015 went far beyond the normal role of grandparenting. In my head, I think I am getting close to acceptance, but in my heart, I am still stuck in anger and tears. My heart will need time to reconcile with my head if I am going to move forward in peace.

How do we heal? I can only heal myself, and healing will take time. Recognizing that fact is huge for me. As much as I would like to rectify the suffering and damage that has occurred over the last five years, I cannot. I especially ache for Crystal, Jim, and Sage, but my other children have suffered as well. The disease of heroin addiction has changed my family forever, and there is no rewind button that will take us back to a simpler time before Crystal put a needle in her arm.

SURRENDER

I told my therapist years ago, after my divorce, that I thought I might be broken. She told me that saying I was broken implied I could not be fixed . . . which wasn't true. I realized that I wasn't broken—I was wounded, and I could heal my wounds. The same is true regarding the last five years. The wounds won't disappear, and the memories will remain, but I believe with time we can patch ourselves up and be better than ever. The suffering and trauma we experienced are now part of who we are, but if we can reconcile those experiences and find forgiveness, they can make us stronger and hopefully more compassionate. Time is the healer, and pain is the catalyst to growth.

Each of my children have taught me things at one time or another. Some of the lessons have not been that much fun, and some have taken multiple teachings for me to finally learn. This summer my eldest daughter has been teaching me about savoring moments and slowing down. She turned forty in May, and I sent her a package with forty individually wrapped gifts. They ranged from gift cards and cash to bubble wands and chocolate bars. Angie loves giving as well as receiving, but when she receives, she does it with focus and gratitude. I would have opened all forty gifts at once, but Angie has taken a full three weeks, appreciating each gift, bow, and wrapping. Allowing Angie to enjoy her gifts at her own pace instead of mine has been a delightful experience, and one I will remember next time I receive a gift.

I am trying to apply this lesson to my current healing. I cannot unwrap all my pain and heartache in one sitting. There will be layers to unfold, and I need to sit with each memory and savor it . . . the good and the bad. If I take my time, I will be able to find gratitude in each step of the journey. The trunk of princess dresses will make me smile and not cry, and the many pictures of Crystal that are still displayed on shelves throughout my house will fill me with good memories and joy.

I cannot heal Crystal or do anything to make her stay clean. That will require Crystal to do the work and determine each day the choices she will make. I will continue praying for her and I will continue loving her. I will be grateful to all the people who made this recovery opportunity a possibility instead of questioning their motives and judging them. I will aim to succeed more days than I fail.

Do I regret bringing Crystal into my life? I've certainly been asked that question on multiple occasions, but the answer is NO. I don't regret bringing any of my children into my life. Crystal was a different kind of choice, and I could have walked away. Instead I walked toward Crystal and embraced her, with all the good and bad, just as I had tried to do with my other children. I didn't do it perfectly, not by any stretch of the imagination, but I did give it my best shot.

For the first few years after Crystal came to live with us, people would ask me if Crystal was grateful that we had taken her in. I would always reply, "I don't know—she acts just as selfish and obnoxious as the rest of my children, so we must be doing something right!" I never wanted Crystal to feel grateful; I only wanted her to feel that we were her family and this was her home. Most of the time I believe she did. I have an abundance of wonderful memories seared into my brain and my heart to remind me of that.

When Crystal was in high school, and only Mick and Max were still living at home, I woke them all up in the middle of the night to go outside and look at some lunar event. I can't

SURRENDER

remember today what the actual event was; it doesn't matter. We grabbed blankets and pillows and went out in the front yard to avoid all the trees and get the best view possible. We spread the blankets on the ground and laid there, just the four of us, looking at the sky, talking and laughing. That is a good memory.

Watching my husband walk her out on the football field at halftime to be crowned homecoming queen, taking pictures before prom—she wore a long blue satin-like skirt and got her hair done up on top of her head—moving her into the dorm in Santa Fe, helping her with her cap and gown before her college graduation, watching her dance—that girl can dance—and holding her child . . . I wouldn't have missed it for anything.

Last week I finally met the reporter from CNN at Starbucks. I knew he had seen Crystal in May when he was putting together the most recent story, and I wanted his take on how she was doing. I also wanted to talk. His reporting had turned my life upside down, but it had also gotten Crystal into rehab. I think it was simply one more step in my healing process. When I told him how hard it had been for me to accept that CNN and a policeman had been able to save Crystal when I couldn't, he had a different perspective. He said that if I had not done what I did over the previous years, it was unlikely they would have ever found Crystal at all. Point taken.

CHAPTER 21

IMPERMANENCE, SORROW, AND LETTING GO

It has been seven months since the first CNN story broke. I am still a work in progress. The media attention, for the most part, has faded. I am working on my sadness and letting go. I have realized that my sadness is simply part of grieving the changes in my life. Instead of stuffing the pain back down, I am trying to embrace it. I do cry, but I also found myself laughing last week over something silly I heard on the radio. There is hope.

I have been listening over and over to *The Art of Living* by Thich Nhat Hanh, the Vietnamese Buddhist monk. The concept of impermanence is hard for me to grasp. I'm one of those people who would prefer that nothing ever change . . . back to my problems with control.

I don't like when my phone updates, I am forced to accept a new operating system on my computer, a television series ends, or a favorite restaurant closes. I have been grieving the change in ownership of my favorite childhood bakery, Casa Linda Bakery, for years now. They made the best birthday cakes I have ever eaten. Actually I am more of an icing person, but you could

SURRENDER

smell a Casa Linda cake when it came in the room and know where it was from. Then it was gone . . . new owners with new recipes. It saved me multiple pounds and broke my heart.

I learned to accept a certain kind of impermanence when Crystal was doing heroin and living on the streets, but that kind of impermanence was based solely on fear—the fear that she would disappear, be killed, or overdose. That impermanence required me to put on armor and guard my heart every day against what "might" happen. I have decided that living in fear is not an acceptable way to live my life. I am trying now to focus on living in the moment and accepting that change occurs with every breath I take.

Thich Nhat Hanh says this about impermanence:

> We are often sad and suffer a lot when things change, but change and **impermanence** have a positive side. Thanks to **impermanence**, everything is possible. . . . If your daughter is not **impermanent**, she cannot grow up to become a woman.

I find this quote reassuring. If Crystal is impermanent, then she can not only grow up to be a woman, but she can grow up to be a sober woman with a future and a passion for living on this amazing planet . . . one day at a time. She can even grow up to be a mother who is able to have a relationship with her daughters.

I know the last two and a half years have changed Crystal, and they have certainly changed me as well. I have a new perspective on the nonsense of life with all its materialism and competitiveness. It all seems so unimportant and trivial now. I think

IMPERMANENCE, SORROW, AND LETTING GO

about the last time I was with Crystal, standing at my door in Dallas as we hugged each other good-bye. I was distracted with work, worried about money, and not focused on the moment. How I wish I could rewind and savor that day in August 2015!

Since Crystal has been in rehab and sober living, we have texted some and have talked on the phone a few times, but she has made no attempt to see me, and that's OK. I spent a lot of words over the years trying to convince Crystal that Jim was a trigger for her addiction, but I understand now that I am a trigger as well. Despite good intentions, I am part of the life that she was living when she started down the road with heroin. I must accept that for Crystal to stay sober and flourish, I may need to back away. I have certainly allowed myself to be codependent in this relationship. Transcribing our text messages for the last few years has made that exceedingly clear!

The positive side of impermanence is that everything is possible. Life is long, and I certainly cannot predict what will occur down the road. I will never be able to understand, on any level, the experiences or the trauma that Crystal went through while living on the streets. I'm sure there were cold and scary nights and loneliness. Days of uncertainty and confusion. I'm sure she felt deserted and forgotten, but I never forgot her, not for a single day.

I also take heart that If nothing is permanent, then I have the prospect of Sage sashaying back into my life and curling up in her butterfly bed with her panda and puppy. They are still there waiting for her.

CHAPTER 22

WE CAN DO BETTER—WE MUST!

I am the lucky one; my child is not dead. Just saying that makes me an anomaly in the current opioid crisis that is ravaging our country. I don't know where Crystal and I will land moving forward in our relationship, but Crystal "IS," and that is the true miracle! The odds were certainly not in her favor. More will die than live in this ongoing epidemic.

I can't imagine that the sequence of events that lined up to save Crystal will ever repeat themselves. I believe that only God could have pulled this one off! There will be other miracles and random "saves"—there always are. I believe we miss most of these chance occurrences as we race through our lives trying to make money and build up our own self-importance. This miracle has changed me, and I hope I can now find a way to help other parents who are living in this nightmare: the nightmare of loving an addict.

Will Crystal stay clean? That part of the story will remain unknown. Philip Seymour Hoffman was sober for twenty-three-years before relapsing. Crystal will need to be vigilant minute by minute and day by day for the rest of her life, but she appears determined.

SURRENDER

Crystal was back in the news this week celebrating six months of sobriety. I'm proud of her. The video replays the past newsreels showing Crystal when she was addicted. Forever online, it's always painful for me to watch. The news clip returns to the present, with Crystal walking with her horse in a beautiful field and talking about her sobriety journey as a shot of the gates of Mending Fences blends into the foreground. It feels more like an ad than a news story. The video cuts to Rebecca and Ryan sitting in a swing, holding Hope and giving an update on their lives and expressing gratitude for Crystal's continued progress. No Tom in this piece.

Crystal is next shown sitting on her bed, a picture of the Holets and Hope prominently featured on the wall beside her. She talks about Rebecca and Ryan as Hope's mother and father and as her family. That hurts, but I am happy she has embraced her adoption decision and can separate from being Hope's mother. That is not an easy thing to do after carrying a baby for nine months. She looks healthy and sounds as articulate as always. Her private school education remains evident. When she opens her mouth to speak, I want to scream, "I paid for those beautiful teeth!"

When I was texting with Crystal last week, she told me she was working on a book. I wasn't surprised, as she had told me earlier that someone had offered to help her write a book recounting her experiences. I mentioned that I was writing as well, in the hope of processing the last five years of her addiction for myself. She texted back that she wasn't sure how she felt about that, but she thought it was "beautiful." I told her I hoped she would write something wonderful that could help others.

Crystal survived on the streets for over two years and is alive and sober to tell about it. She has a rare opportunity to offer perspective and make a difference in the lives of other addicts. I hope that by sharing her experiences, she can save someone else from going down the same road, and I pray she can stay sober in the process. We are walking in a world where no one appears to have a workable solution to the opioid problem. Any light Crystal can shine from the addict's perspective can only be positive.

As Crystal persists along her road to recovery, I continue down mine. I have no cures or words of wisdom to offer the multitude of struggling addicts, and I have no magic answers to the opioid crisis. I'm just a mother stumbling down her own path. By writing about my journey, I can only hope to offer something to other parents of addicts and remind them that they are not alone. There are no black-and-white answers here! The internet, on the other hand, is full of advice on what you should and shouldn't do. Most of what I found there I already knew, but it was nice to know I wasn't the only one trying to figure it out. Here is what I've learned:

Parents are enablers. I got a gold star for that one!

We can't fix our addicts. That concept was much easier to accept in my mind than in my heart, and I continued to try multiple solutions of my own. I don't think I accepted that I couldn't fix Crystal until someone else stepped in and it was no longer an option for me.

Addicts break the hearts of their parents and those who love them. I read over and over that addicts are liars and criminals who show no remorse. As I've gone through text messages, arrest records, and emails for the last few years, I can see how accurate that statement is, but I've also received text messages that showed genuine remorse and care, and I believe they are also true.

You cannot force your addict to get clean. The addict you are trying so desperately to save is no longer the child you knew and nurtured. As long as your addict is using, they are not hearing your pleas and tears. I offered rehab multiple times over the years. I had no idea how I would pay for treatment or the best place for her to go, but I offered. The resources for reliable information are quite limited. In the end, Crystal was never willing to take a serious step toward getting clean until a policeman found her in the alley with a needle in her arm. She was the only one who could make the decision to get clean.

Your addict is not doing this to hurt you; they are just doing it. Crystal was struggling and in pain. The grip that heroin had on my sweet girl was tortuous to watch on every level. I never thought for even a moment that she was doing this to hurt me. Crystal suffered the most. My pain was collateral damage.

Having an addict in your life is isolating. When you have a heroin addict in your life, it is hard to relate to even your closest friends. I was living my life on the edge of my seat waiting for the call that Crystal had overdosed or was in jail. My life was unpredictable, and the fact that I was constantly dealing with an unstable person kept me spinning. It became easier to be by myself, but that was lonely. The longer it went on, the more isolated I became. To be fair to my friends, I wasn't much fun, and I didn't ask for their help.

WE CAN DO BETTER—WE MUST!

This is what I believe must change. When your child is a heroin addict, no one knows what to say, but I found that I wasn't looking for friends to say anything. I needed someone who would listen without trying to fix the situation. It sounds simple, but it's a tough thing to ask. We seem programmed to talk more than listen. I know I'm working on that. Listening compassionately to another person's struggles is a form of true healing for the one pouring out their pain.

Addiction is a disease. People differ in their opinions on addiction being a disease or a choice, but I have watched my daughter, and I cannot imagine that anyone would voluntarily choose what she has gone through. My belief that addiction is a disease helps me to put one foot in front of the other and conceive of the possibility for hope and healing.

People judge. Parents of addicts isolate for good reason. The first few times I told people that my daughter was a heroin addict living on the streets, they looked at me like I was Cruella de Ville. First they wanted to know what "living on the streets" really meant. It was sad in a funny way. When I explained that she was sleeping under a bridge or in a park, sometimes in a tent or staying with others, they stared at me with a "deer in the headlight" look in their eyes and had nothing to say. Those who have not experienced having a drug addict in their lives cannot comprehend it, and worse, they make you feel terrible about yourself. No wonder parents don't talk about it.

I hope that as more and more parents come forward with their stories, people will replace their judgment with empathy and support. And if they can't do that, I hope they

SURRENDER

will remember the old saying, "If you can't say anything nice, don't say anything at all." A simple "I'm sorry you're going through this" is enough.

You can't go back, and you must let go. Crystal and I cannot go back; there are no "do-overs." Life before heroin is gone. If Crystal stays sober, our new reality offers some hope for forgiveness, reconciliation, and freedom. For Crystal, it's freedom from the drug that destroyed her old life and a chance to begin again. For me, it's freedom from my obsession with Crystal and fixing her addiction.

I want to believe I have fully forgiven Crystal, but the knot in my stomach tells me I still have work to do. I will continue praying and trudging toward healing one day at a time. I love Crystal. This love is a blind emotion that doesn't go away once you fully accept a child into your life as your own. If letting Crystal go is the best way for her to stay sober and create a new life, I love her enough to do that. Life is long, and reconciliation can be just over the next ridge.

WE CAN DO BETTER—WE MUST!

So, to my daughter I say:

"I love you, Crystal. Be strong and let God guide your footsteps. Do the work to stay sober and heal others along the way. Find a way to reconcile with your daughter; she needs a mother, but only a fully sober one. Open your eyes to the light and joy this life has to offer, and know that I always carry you in my heart.
Love always, Mamma"

July 18, 2017

EPILOGUE

FROM CRYSTAL

I must confess that when I read this real-life tale of a mother struggling to get a grasp on her daughter's addiction to heroin, it was immensely humbling. Reading a book written about a parent's experience with their child's addictive recourse bombarded me with intense and powerful memories of the past. I made a small attempt at reading this story like it was written about someone else. Instead I stand in my truth. Fortunately for me, I happen to be the main character of this insightful nonfiction. I use the word fortunate because my perspective has changed.

Hi, my name is Crystal, and I am an addict.

The past year has been a life-changing experience. Call it the stars aligning or call it fate, whatever the case may be, it has definitely transformed my soul. Although I am now in recovery, the fact of the matter is that my loved ones suffered an incredible loss when I picked up my first drug.

Recalling memories of the younger me, I don't wish to warn her about the disease of addiction, how it would almost end my life. I do, however, yearn to warn my loved ones of the overwhelming course of destruction that would inevitably impact their lives in ways not yet imagined, and how action could be taken to prevent this. Nevertheless, if they had educated themselves on the dark side of this disease, there is no guarantee that anything would have been different. Until an addict makes the decision to change their own life, it's nothing more than fools' wisdom. To quote the great French novelist, Marcel Proust: "We don't receive wisdom; we must discover it for ourselves after a journey that no one can take for us, or spare us."

Although I now abstain from all drugs and alcohol and, more importantly, work a solid program in recovery, the devastating road I paved took years of construction from a life in active addiction. One of the dire consequences has been the sheer selfishness that my disease demanded of me, thus hurting anyone and everyone that attempted to love me and stand by my side through any given part of the last eighteen years.

Whether this is a positive or a negative is not up to me to decide. What I can decide is how I spend the rest of my days on this planet. While I know my story is proof of divine intervention and hope, this disease breeds a torturing, complex beast that affects countless lives. On the flip side of addiction is recovery, which takes an honest desire to change one's life, determination, and hard work via action and the belief in a higher power.

The only permanent in life is death, yet we are all here on this planet to live, learn, grow, and most importantly to love, unconditionally at that. Love is what changed my life; it's as simple as that. Unconditional love and support was given by two perfect strangers, once at age fifteen and once again at age thirty-five. It was a reminder for me in my darkest moments, changing my life's circumstance for the greater good. I wholeheartedly

EPILOGUE

believe that an immersion in loving compassion is the only successful way to help someone with this disease.

James A. Garfield once said, "The truth will set you free, but first it will make you miserable."

Recovery is a journey. In the school of life, I have learned to take care of my mind, body, and most importantly, my spirit. How have I accomplished this? Simple, I got honest and then put action behind my truth, and this takes time.

First, I went through the physical and emotional growing pains of early sobriety, with the aid and assistance of a number of kind souls in the business of helping people specifically with the disease of addiction. Opening my mind and heart and changing my perspective came next. It became the utmost necessity to change my thought patterns, which in turn changed my perspective. I had to wake up to the past patterns and the self-fulfilling prophecies that landed me chained to my disease. Then came forgiveness.

The subconscious part of our human brain is incredibly intelligent and illuminating; it leads the way. What I mean by this is that our subconscious listens and pays the most accurate of attention to everything we think and feel. If this is a fact (and it is), then if I am constantly feeding my subconscious negative thoughts while not living in my truth, it will organically make all the negative a reality. Now that I am in recovery, I work constantly on living in my truth while remaining open-minded. Lastly, I am committed to working a twelve-step program.

Now don't get me wrong, my "humanness" does get in the way, and it will continue to get in the way. This is where acceptance and humility take center stage. Those living with this disease will continue to suffer until they get honest and begin to accept their faults, forgive themselves, live in their truth, and make amends with the past. On the flip side, I am now capable of helping others with this plight—while remaining teachable, always. This is a disease of the spirit. The overwhelming fear and feeling of doom on top of whatever trauma, pain, and suffering happens in our lives holds an incredible amount of weight on someone in active addiction.

I need all the help I can get, yet like anything in life, it is a practice. The practice gets easier and easier, and more connections are made. However, the practice must be done to accomplish the end goal: living a life free from addiction.

Navigating this life in recovery and knowing in my heart that I never have to be alone again opens a whole new world of opportunities. Only I have the ability to make the decision. Once we understand that we only control ourselves and therefore are responsible for our emotions, then the healing will begin. This is truth.

Life is painful. Pain is a feeling all humans experience, and pleasure would not exist without it. Pain also holds the capacity to manifest character traits that embellish the dark side of life. Fear, ego, and false pride all run wild when we do not accept the outside world exactly as it is. A victim mentality ensues when we think and believe the world has done us wrong. Living a life in recovery means that I had to accept the wrongs that happened to me, using these wrongs for momentum while challenging my fears.

The good news is that there is a way out; there is always hope. Living with the disease of addiction is like living with any other type of disease. There are serious consequences if one does not utilize the abundant amount of resources available for treatment. The difference lies in the fact that those of us with addictive personalities end up addicted to substances because we are attempting to self-medicate from the pain of life's traumas. On top of that, once a sick and suffering human is in the vicious cycle of addiction, isolated and alone, it's like being in a prison of their own making. The hard truth is that the only person who has any control over these consequences is the addict himself.

If we are going to change the stereotype of addiction, our culture needs a shift in perspective. Resources need to be more affordable and education on the subject readily available. I was one of the lucky ones. Both times I went to rehab and detox were paid for by state funding and scholarships. Opioid addiction is currently an epidemic. If you are reading this, my hope is that you have been educated. What you do with this information is up to you. For me personally, I have been blessed with the purpose to do whatever is in my power to help those affected by this crisis.

There are six regular actions I take to keep my demons at bay. I attend regular meetings of a twelve-step program; I stay accountable with certain individuals (my life advisors); I sponsor others with the same disease; and I pray, meditate, and run on a regular basis. The bottom line is that I take care of my mind, body, and spirit. This would not be possible if I hadn't done the work on my real issues of codependency and trauma from my past.

Gratefully, I am sober today and that is what I focus on: the present. Life is happening right here, right now. It is hands down the greatest gift I have ever been given. It takes a village; it takes open discussions; and we all must work together for the greater good to fight against this disease.

SURRENDER

I invite you to put your judgments aside and keep an open mind. Through kindness, compassion, and unconditional love, you may just change someone's life.

www.ingramcontent.com/pod-product-compliance
Lightning Source LLC
Chambersburg PA
CBHW052054110526
44591CB00013B/2208